2004 P

ONCE UPON A RHYME

IMAGINATION FOR
A NEW GENERATION

Poems From
Lancashire Vol II
Edited by Steve Twelvetree

Young **Writers**

First published in Great Britain in 2005 by:
Young Writers
Remus House
Coltsfoot Drive
Peterborough
PE2 9JX
Telephone: 01733 890066
Website: www.youngwriters.co.uk

SB ISBN 1 84460 689 9

Foreword

Young Writers was established in 1991 and has been passionately devoted to the promotion of reading and writing in children and young adults ever since. The quest continues today. Young Writers remains as committed to engendering the fostering of burgeoning poetic and literary talent as ever.

This year's Young Writers competition has proven as vibrant and dynamic as ever and we are delighted to present a showcase of the best poetry from across the UK. Each poem has been carefully selected from a wealth of *Once Upon A Rhyme* entries before ultimately being published in this, our twelfth primary school poetry series.

Once again, we have been supremely impressed by the overall high quality of the entries we have received. The imagination, energy and creativity which has gone into each young writer's entry made choosing the best poems a challenging and often difficult but ultimately hugely rewarding task - the general high standard of the work submitted amply vindicating this opportunity to bring their poetry to a larger appreciative audience.

We sincerely hope you are pleased with our final selection and that you will enjoy *Once Upon A Rhyme Poems From Lancashire Vol II* for many years to come.

Contents

Estcourt Preparatory School

Bhakti Amin (9)	14
Nicole Wilkinson (10)	15
Shannon Westwood (9)	16
Arusa Rasool (10)	16
April Tsang (9)	17
Emma Stewart (10)	17
Jessica Greenwood (9)	18
Sarah Bates (11)	19
Olivia Torr (10)	19
Rebecca Rooney (10)	20
Ashleigh Cruse (9)	20
Morgan Prescott (10)	21
Rea Patel (10)	21
Heather Lacey (10)	22
Sahrish Qasim (10)	22
Alexandra Nield (9)	23
Lucy Bradley (10)	24
Danielle Wildbore (9)	24
Natalie Newton (10)	25
Charlotte Tilley (10)	25
Emma Taylor (10)	26
Lauren Lockett (10)	27
Natalie Agarwal (9)	28
Gabrielle Rhodes (10)	28
Helen Gourley (9)	29
Georgia Hicks (9)	30
Grace Holland (10)	30
Poppy Robinson (9)	31
Laura Ferns (10)	31
Danielle Riley (10)	32
Olivia Ketley (10)	32
Rachael Bolton (9)	33
Emma Sibson (10)	34
Mariam Ahmed (9)	35
Bianca Crisci (10)	36
Sophie Smith (9)	37
Chloe Shaw (10)	38
Lauren Cunliffe (10)	38
Eleanor Wild (9)	39
Shradha Amin (9)	40
Lucy Crossland (9)	41

Hulme Court Preparatory School

James Laing (9)	66
Jack Mansley (10)	67
Ben Campbell (9)	67
James Fisher (8)	68
Matthew McDonald (9)	68
Robert Thackeray (9)	68
George Littler-Hyde (10)	69
Nikesh Mistry (9)	69
James Foy (10)	70
Jake Riley (9)	70
Benjamin Chorlton-Kerans (9)	70
Luke Butler (10)	71
Jack Lawrence (9)	71
Sammi Chekroud (9)	72
Daniel Fielding (9)	72
Robert Smillie (10)	73
Calvin Wong (9)	73
Akshay Gulati (9)	74
Joseph Furness (9)	74
Joshua Williams (10)	75
Rakibul Huda (10)	75
Thomas Russell (11)	76
Luke Kirkham (9)	76
Thomas Clements (10)	77
Sam Alexander Mellor (9)	77
Sheik Raja (11)	78
James Craughwell (10)	78
Ameen Chekroud (9)	79
Daniel Murphy (10)	79
Alex Claydon (11)	80
Luqman Mehboob (11)	80
Shamas Qumar (10)	81
Matthew Stocker (11)	81
Ryan Ellis (10)	82
Andrew Schofield (10)	82
Joshua Sayle (10)	83
Chris Claydon (9)	83
Christopher Whitworth (10)	84
William Lacey (10)	84
Naqash Matloob (10)	85

Jonathan Lobley (9)   85

Limehurst CP School
Charley Bezzina (7)   86
Luke Davies (8)   86
Emily Atherton (8)   87
Aiden Kelly (8)   87

Marsden CP School
Charlotte Laskey (10)   88
Farah Araf (10)   88
Kasim Hussain (10)   89
Sidra Alyas (10)   89
Saresh Ilyas (10)   90
Saana Ilyas (11)   90
Asim Ahmed (10)   91
Isaaq Mohammed (10)   91
Usman Khan (10)   92
Sophia Rehman (10)   93
Shahjahan Aslam (10)   93
Hassan Mahmood (10)   94
Ryan Richmond (10)   94
Adnan Hussain (10)   95
Kathryn Evans (10)   95
Ibrahim Mahmood (10)   96
Sufyan Iqbal (10)   96
Mehvish Khan (10)   97
Sabah Kiani (10)   97

Our Lady's RC Primary School
Michael Owen (10)   97
Jordan Wood (10)   98
Thomas Gray (10)   98
Laura Holmes (10)   98
Christian Jacobs (9)   99
Patrick Smith (9)   99
Helen Richards (10)   100
Charlotte Taylor (10)   100
Caitlin O'Ryan (9)   101
Jess Willcock (10)   101

Richard Durning's Endowed Primary School

Molly Beswick (10)	102
Emily Turner (10)	102
George Warburton (10)	103
Emily Cassell (10)	103
Rachael Garner (10)	104
Tom Cowin (10)	105
Louise Bowyer (9)	106
Emily Kingsford (10)	106
Samantha Welch (10)	107
Isabel Kingsford (9)	108
Laura Miller (9)	108
Lydia Tomlinson (9)	109
Jessica Moir (9)	109
Laura Preece (9)	110
Harriet Bowyer (9)	111
Jack Garner (10)	112
Natalie Eccles (9)	112

St John's Catholic Primary School, Burscough

Eleanor Parker (7)	113
Georgina Pritchard (8)	113
Alexandra Till (8)	113
Emma Forshaw (8)	114
Hannah Wilson (8)	114
Maria Mir (8)	115
Muneeb Mir (7)	115

St Mark's CE Primary School, Wigan

Catherine Stevens (10)	116
Tanya Ratcliffe (10)	116
Bethany Sharkey (10)	117
Thomas Janetis (10)	117
Chelsea Dempsey (10)	118
Lucy Jennion (10)	118
Annya Stafford (10)	119
Amy Sutton (10)	119
Georgina O'Leary (11)	120
Matthew Cottle (10)	120
Adam Corless (10)	121
Lauren Shaw (10)	122

St Peter's CE Primary School, Heysham

Emily Pearce (8)	136
Erica Pitcher (8)	136
Carly Beckwith (8)	137
Darcy Giles (8)	137
Literacy Group 5	138
Jessica Fenton (8)	138
Richard Bell (7)	138
Jennifer Knowles (7)	139
Kate Rogers (7)	139
Matthew Guest (7)	139
Katy Bates (8)	140
Emma Hutchinson (8)	140

St Philip's RC Primary School, Salford

Michael Mottram (7)	141
Niamh Hickey (7)	141
Lucy Whittaker (7)	142
Kellen Welch (7)	142
Megan Mitchell (7)	143
Liam Peers (7)	143
Sean Doran (7)	143
Mason Considine (7)	144
Charlotte White (7)	144
Jessica Wilcock (8)	144
Isabelle Kemp (10)	145
Alexander Mayers (7)	145
Nicola Cuddy (10)	146
Salvatore Briffa (10)	146
Emily Litchfield (7)	146
Lewis Conlan (7)	147
Tito Okanlami (7)	148
Annie Rose Hanily (7)	148
Victoria Ejgierd (7)	148
Molly Stockton (11)	149
Rachel Kinlin (10)	149
Áine Hughes (9)	150
Luke Bolton (8)	150
Dominique O'Kane (10)	151
Cheta Anyanwa (10)	151
Fionnuala Feeney (7)	152

Paul Coughlin (9)   196

Sacred Heart Catholic Primary School
Laura Elford-O'Dowd (10)   197
Charmaine Johnson (10)   197
Joseph Jolly (10)   198
Charles Iddon (10)   198
Victoria Tootell (10)   199
Lucy Parkinson (10)   199
Nicola Blackledge (10)   200
Bethany McMullan (10)   200
Leah Westwater (10)   201
Shannon Jones (10)   201
Stephen Sumner (11)   201
Henry Linn (10)   202

Singleton CE Primary School
Toby Gratrix (7)   202
Bethany Tomlinson (10)   202
Josh Powlesland (10)   203
Greg Richardson (10)   203
Katie Davies (9)   204
Harry Heywood (9)   204
Lauren Taziker (10)   205
Lucy Hilton (10)   205
Jordan Leighton (10)   206
Jamie Fish (10)   206
Laura Wood (10)   207
Victoria Birkett (10)   207
Richard Booth (9)   208
Hattie Pridmore (10)   208
Rebecca Macdonald (11)   209
Lawrence Berry (10)   209
Samuel Sandham (8)   210
Rhianne Wilson (10)   210
Jordan Bamber (8)   210
Emily Barrett (9)   211
Emma Dewhurst (8)   211
Dan Collins (8)   211
Lucy Willman (8)   212
Paul Fretwell (8)   212

Ruby Gratrix (8)   212
Christian Powlesland (7)   213
Lily Jackson (8)   213
Charlotte Mowbray (8)   213
Ross Macdonald (11)   214

Todmorden CE Primary School
Harriot Whelan (10)   214
Sophie Mitchell (10)   215
Carl Blakely (10)   215
Barry Cooper (10)   216
Jacob Lomax (10)   217
Dannielle Westney (10)   218
Ian Gardiner (10)   218
Jacob Colclough (10)   219
Isaac Pearson (10)   219
Bethany Whitcombe (10)   219
Eve Brandon (10)   220
Jamie Crampton (10)   220
Jack Garbett (10)   221
Jordan Hudson (10)   221
Sophie Lord (10)   222
Megan McGuinn (10)   222
Billy McCubbin & Matthew Goldthorpe (10)   223

Trinity & St Michael's CE Primary School
Jodie Bamford (10)   223
William Booth (10)   224
Joe Grice (7)   224
Robbie Pilcher (9)   225
Aaron Jordan (7)   225
Lyndsey Smart (10)   226
Meghann Cheetham (8)   227
Victoria Bate (11)   227

Winmarleigh CE School
Matthew Parker (10)   228
Andrew Young (8)   228
Jack Swindlehurst (9)   229
Benjamin Parker (8)   229

The Poems

The Seasons

Spring
Spring is when baby animals are being born,
Flowers growing in fields and in gardens,
Easter time when you get Easter eggs.

Summer
Summer is when the holidays start
With the clear blue seas,
When sunflowers start to grow,
Beautiful sunsets.

Autumn
Autumn is when baby animals start to grow up,
Wind is growing stronger and stronger,
The leaves changing colour,
Brown, orange, green, red and gold.

Winter
Winter is when icicles are hanging from the garden gnomes,
Snowmen being built in the park,
Snow drifting from the sky,
Wrap up warm when you go outside.

Jessica Parker (10)
Adlington Primary School

Anger

Anger is black, like a dark haunted forest.
I hear people yelling down my ear.
The scent of smoke from people's cigarettes hanging around me.
All I can see is mist and nothing else.
I feel as though I am trapped in a cold wet box.
It reminds me of loneliness.

Naomi Gent (10)
Adlington Primary School

Anger

Anger is a deep rage which makes you want to kill people.
Anger is a fire in your belly that comes out in your face as
a scorching hot volcano.
It is a firework shooting into the night sky, burning and
ready to explode.
Anger is the scent of hate drifting up my nose.
It's the sight of a decomposing body, with no chance to live again.
Anger is blood oozing out of a sliced hand.
It reminds me of bad memories and I have no hope to forget them.

James Welch (11)
Adlington Primary School

Anger

Anger is red, like a bonfire lighting up the night sky,
It is like thunder echoing through the valley,
Anger is like the smell of some rotting body of an animal.

Anger is lightning hitting a space probe on its way down to Earth,
It is like being betrayed by friends and family
Or reminding me of bad memories.

Dominic Entwistle (11)
Adlington Primary School

Anger

Anger is red like a fierce explosion in a quarry.
Anger is the sound of a pedestrian riot on the streets.
Anger is the smell of flesh scorching in a fire.
Anger is the sight of a corpse lying in the desert.
Anger is the feel of jagged rocks at the beach.
Anger reminds me of blood oozing from a wolf's victim.

Thomas Curwood-Cameron (9)
Adlington Primary School

The Seasons

Spring is full of blossom,
It is warm sunny days,
Everyone is enjoying their Easter eggs,
Birds are singing in the trees.

Summer is sausages sizzling on the barbecue,
It is travelling to the airport to go on holiday,
Summer is sitting on the beach and getting a tan,
It is eating cold, melting ice cream.

Autumn is standing on brown, crunchy leaves,
It is watching a bonfire burning through the night,
Autumn is waking up to cloudy mornings,
It is sitting next to the warm fire.

Winter is enjoying Christmas,
It is waking up to white, snowy mornings,
Eating turkey for your Christmas dinner,
Winter is a time to hibernate.

Kayleigh Delaney (10)
Adlington Primary School

Anger

Anger is red like a blazing fire,
Or a venomous spider waiting to inject its venom.
Anger is the sound of a woman screeching
And a poisonous snake hissing at its prey.
Anger is the smell of a troll's breath
And a skunk's rotten smell.

Anger looks like someone getting beaten,
A scorpion stinging with its tail.
Anger feels like poison running through my veins,
Blood dripping down my arm.
Anger reminds me of someone suffering,
Or something dying in pain.

Daniel Atherton (11)
Adlington Primary School

The Seasons

Spring
Spring is a garden of flowers bursting into bloom
A time when lambs are born in lush green fields
The bare, brown trees turning green
Animals starting to come out of hibernation

Summer
Summer is when people can enjoy the beautiful sun setting at night
A swimming pool rippling in someone's back garden
Butterflies and bees fluttering about and collecting pollen

Autumn
Autumn is when the weather goes cold
And the leaves crumple beneath my feet
When the daffodils start to die
Because winter is on its way

Winter
Winter is when the nights grow dark early in the evening
A time when children look forward to Christmas
When the snow falls leaving the hillsides beautiful and white.

Megan Jones (11)
Adlington Primary School

Anger

Anger is red, like a bonfire burning brightly in the night.
Anger is the sound of people in your mind,
The smell of rotten sandwiches which your mum has put up for dinner.

The sight of a football when you have shot and missed,
Anger is when you feel a rock-hard stone with its roughness,
Anger reminds me of when people pick on you
And you want to hit them back but you do not have the courage.

Dominic Aspinall (9)
Adlington Primary School

Seasons

Spring is when flowers are starting to come into bloom
Or the sun heating up the lush grass
Newborn lambs gambolling around the field

Summer is when people relax in their gardens
When ice cream dribbles down your top
Or the waves beating on the shore

Autumn is when leaves convert to brown
When they crackle beneath your feet
And when the breeze starts to go nippy

Winter is when the snow drifts through the air
When people's fires gleam in cosy houses
Or when the scent of the Christmas tree circulates in your house.

Lee Cook (11)
Adlington Primary School

I Am . . .

I am a monkey hanging on trees,
I am a butterfly in the breeze,
I am a silky, purple coat,
I am a hairy, smelly goat.

I am a lovely chicken kebab,
I am a nasty, nipping crab,
I am a tasty toffee,
I am a cup of coffee.

I am a Christmas tree,
I am a bumbling bee,
I am a sparkling car,
I am a chocolate bar.

Bethaney Walkden (9)
Adlington Primary School

I Am . . .

I am a bee sitting on a calm petal,
I am a flower swaying in the grass
Or a fly, shining by the light.

I am a red rose prickling someone's finger,
I am an autumn leaf falling to the ground
Or a bud opening to a new life.

I am a daisy being trampled on,
I am a dull log dead on the ground
Or a branch being snapped.

Chelsey Makinson (9)
Adlington Primary School

Fear

Fear is grey like a stone.
Fear is like being blinded in a haunted house.
Fear tastes like salt, you have to spit it out.
It sounds like your heart's bumping.
It feels as if you have been hit by a car.
It smells like blood.
It looks like a ghost.
It reminds me of dead people.

Ellie Wilkinson (7)
Bolton-by-Bowland CE Primary School

Happiness

Happiness is pale blue like the clear sky.
Happiness sounds like the waves crashing.
Happiness tastes like fair trade chocolate.
Happiness smells like spring flowers.
Happiness looks like a golden sun shining.
Happiness reminds me of my hamster when I first got her.

Katy Greenwood (7)
Bolton-by-Bowland CE Primary School

My Ponies, Harry And Blossom

My ponies, Harry and Blossom,
Well, Blossom has quite a big, fat bottom.
She can whinny for the world,
She even jumps her stable door.

My ponies, Harry and Blossom,
Well, Harry has the loveliest trot.
He can run for the world,
But when he gets his dinner he turns into the silliest pony ever!

My two pones, Harry and Blossom,
They're the cheekiest ones I've seen,
They hide in the field when I'm outside,
But they're the most loving creatures you could keep.

Annabelle Davenport (8)
Bolton-by-Bowland CE Primary School

Happiness

Happiness is blue like the sea.
Happiness sounds like a musical piano.
Happiness tastes like lemon pancakes.
Happiness smells like spring flowers.
Happiness looks like golden raindrops.
Happiness reminds me of my holidays.

Jamie Howson (7)
Bolton-by-Bowland CE Primary School

Favourite Things

I like to drink banana milkshake,
Especially with banana ice cream.
I like to play with my PlayStation 1,
I'm going to get an Xbox too.
I love to play chess and draughts,
Especially when I get fish and chips for tea!

Angus Wilson (7)
Bolton-by-Bowland CE Primary School

Our Dog, Penny

Our dog, Penny, is the best,
She is a Jack Russell,
She is white and black on her back,
She is light brown on her face.

Our dog, Penny, wanders around the farm,
Which can be rather a pain in the arm,
She chases cats and rats,
But she doesn't care.

Our dog, Penny, is a lovely little dog,
I'll love her forever and ever,
I'll never ever let her go,
She's our little dog, that's our dog, Penny.

Laura Barron (8)
Bolton-by-Bowland CE Primary School

Our Puppy, Bella

Our puppy, Belly is a pain in the arm,
She is sometimes so cute,
But she does a lot of harm.
She is black and white,
With two black patches round her eyes,
When we go to school she says her goodbyes.

Kate Robinson (8)
Bolton-by-Bowland CE Primary School

Fear

Fear is peach for the pale skin
Fear sounds like people killing each other
Fear tastes like sour milk left in the sun
Fear smells like blood from the injured ones
Fear looks like people dead on the floor
Fear reminds me of those who fought in the war.

Marcus Blackwell (8)
Bolton-by-Bowland CE Primary School

I Love Gem!

I've got a dog called Gem,
She's the cutest dog around,
She licks and plays with everyone,
Cos Gem is number one.

My puppy, Gem
Is brown and white.
She loves to bark and play around,
To me she is worth a million pounds.

Emma Simpson (10)
Bolton-by-Bowland CE Primary School

Anger

Anger is red like a red-faced person
with steam coming out of their ears!
It sounds like a steam train running
round your head.
It tastes like a really, really hot vindaloo.
It smells like rotting, dead rats.
It looks like waste food in the bin.
It reminds me of when I lose a huge fish.

Calum Harris (9)
Bolton-by-Bowland CE Primary School

Happiness

Happiness is yellow like the sun shining,
Happiness sounds like parties and fun,
Happiness tastes like toffee sweets,
Happiness smells like chocolate cakes,
Happiness looks like joy and toys to play with,
Happiness reminds me of my second birthday.

Naomi Collinson (9)
Bolton-by-Bowland CE Primary School

Months

January is for the snow, so deep.
February is for the fog, too thick to see through.
March is for the weak and feeble sun.
April is for the showers, long and short.
May is for the bright flowers, big and small.
June is for the leaves, so green and rich.
July is for the strong summer sun.
August is for the holidays, camping and caravanning.
September is for the colours of the leaves, brown, red and
                                        much, much more.
October is for the days growing ever shorter and shorter.
November is for the frost and the night, so cold and black.
December is for Christmas, so many trees and lights.
It's my favourite time of year!

Matthew Wilkinson (9)
Bolton-by-Bowland CE Primary School

Bella, The Muddy Pup

Our puppy, Bella, is black and white,
She's the best puppy alright.
She likes barking and likes her tea,
She loves to chase but comes back all muddy.

She likes chasing cats
And she jumps up at bats,
Yes, she is the best
But a little bit of a pest.

She chews up anything she can find,
But she brings you things, she's very kind.
She does not like the rain,
But everyone loves her all the same,
That's our puppy, Bella!

Hannah Robinson (11)
Bolton-by-Bowland CE Primary School

Hate

The colour of hate is
blacky-red like a bonfire.
It sounds like raging
thunder in my head.
It tastes like burnt chips.
It smells like burnt sausages.
It looks like a black
thundercloud.
It reminds me of wild horses
charging after me.

Ben Eccles (9)
Bolton-by-Bowland CE Primary School

Sadness

Sadness is grey like a slow lumbering elephant.
Sadness sounds like a child crying.
Sadness tastes like dry sand.
Sadness smells of thick, black smoke.
Sadness looks like a wet, windy night.
Sadness reminds me of war and guns firing constantly.

James Robinson (9)
Bolton-by-Bowland CE Primary School

Happiness

Happiness is bright like warm sunny days.
It sounds like happy chirping birds.
It tastes like sweet melted chocolate.
It smells like new blossom on a tree.
It looks like a hill of flowers.
It reminds me of my birthday.

Alexander Guthrie (10)
Bolton-by-Bowland CE Primary School

Starry Sky

The stars are a princess
Gleaming, shining, sparkling
Always there at night

The moon is her prince
Together they dance
Or sing a love song

But when the moon is far away
The stars begin to cry
But she knows he'll always come back
And stay forever and always.

Rachael Heery (10)
Delphside Community Primary School

Snowman

There was a wizard
In a blizzard
Who wanted to make a man
He swished his wand around
To see what he could do
The man appeared
White and cold
He melted in a week.

David Johannessen (8)
Delphside Community Primary School

Sunset

S unset burning bright
U nder the deep blue sky
N earer and nearer
S inking through the sky
E scaping cracks in the clouds
T ime to go, bye-bye.

Charlotte Leigh (10)
Delphside Community Primary School

The Everlasting River

It was a lovely time, a time that is long gone.
I ran through fields, where cattle drank from my crystal clear shine.
I crashed into rocks, as I swiftly whizzed down waterfalls.
Softly, I flowed through woods.
Trickled like a tap down hillsides.
Butterflies, who came to drink, tickled my wavy skin.
Bunny rabbits hopped playfully on the bank, whilst birds sang
                                        beautifully up in the trees.
An abundance of bluebells grew like a huge garden of aqua lanterns.
Apples fell from the trees like bullets.
Flowers of all different shades surrounded me.
As the sun shone in the sky, the beams gave life to everything.
The golden leaves that fell on me I wear like awards that
                                        shine in the light.
As the sun came down and the moon came up, I crept quietly
                                        under the burning stars.
The racoons who came to drink used their velvet paws to
                                        scoop up the water.
The moon's reflection shone into me and made everyone calm.
But from that day on, it all changed.
Brick after brick they built big tall towers over me.
Huge yellow monsters dug me up.
Everyone who lived in me scattered away scared.
From that day I have become gardens, houses and other buildings.
That's my sad broken story.

Naomi Bond (10)
Delphside Community Primary School

Crocodiles

Crocodiles are greedy
Crocodiles are speedy
Their eyes are beady

Crocodiles are long
Crocodiles are strong
Crocodiles live in a pond

Crocodiles are big
Crocodiles always dig
A crocodile ate a pig.

Kieran Wall (9)
Delphside Community Primary School

Embarrassed

It was my school play
And I was so embarrassed
So shall I tell you
What happened on that day?

As it began
My friend went on stage
She tripped over and fell
So we had to start again!

When I went on stage
I pretended to go in a house
When a spider ran up my legs
I squeaked like a mouse!

When we had finished
A person came backstage
When they opened the door
We were getting changed!

That was my embarrassing day
So don't you *dare* do the same!

Bhakti Amin (9)
Estcourt Preparatory School

Teacher's Pet!

My pet is so calm and tame
Pip is my dog's name, you see!
For my pet dog is better than a frog
A bat or chimpanzee!

The teachers in my school must think
They're working in a zoo
Their classrooms feature many a creature
Here are just a few

Madame Bloggs keeps pet frogs
She says they're good for kissing
But what we really want to know
Is why their legs are missing?

Miss Li has a chimpanzee
It leaps about and wriggles
It pulls her hair and thumps her chair
And gives us all the giggles

Mrs Maitland has a bat called Caitlan
It smiles with teeth that bite
When it's time for sums, it shows its gums
And helps us get them right!

The weather got drier and hotter
Which was bad for Mrs Schofield's otter
The swimming pool looked refreshing and cool
But we had to jump in and not her!

Mrs Fleming so calming and charming
Has the best pet there can be
I hope she gets no other pet
For Mrs Fleming's pet is *me!*

Nicole Wilkinson (10)
Estcourt Preparatory School

Spirit

Spirit leader of the Cimarron heard
A brave and noble mustang
He stands bold watching over his homeland
Head held high so proud and strong

His coat is golden and smooth
His mane is as black as the night
As he gallops across the plains
His eyes sparkle like stars in the moonlight

Spirit's homeland is a beautiful place
With clear blue skies and deep rock canyons
Tall pine trees grow in the mountains
And fast-flowing rivers run though the valleys

Under the starry sky at night
This beautiful stallion watches over his homeland
Making sure that everything is fine
So no enemies will sneak past him

His patient and loving mother, Kiara
A beautiful and brave palomino mare
Taught her son to defend himself
And fight against his enemies.

Shannon Westwood (9)
Estcourt Preparatory School

Colours

Red, blue, orange, green,
There are lots of colours I have seen,
Silver, gold, purple, pink,
Lots of colours all in a link,
White, brown, grey and violet,
Some colours you can see when you're up high as a pilot,
Yellow, black and aqua too,
Let's all sing a rhyme or two.

Arusa Rasool (10)
Estcourt Preparatory School

My Mum's The Best!

My mum is the best!
She always tidies my bed
She's very good at playing chess
That's why she is the best!

She's always nice and playful
She's never, never dull
She's the coolest mother
I wouldn't change for any other

Her smile makes me smile too
That's why I'm never blue
She teaches me the right from wrong
And makes me feel strong

My mum is very kind
She is quite hard to find
Her skin is so soft to touch
So that's why I love her so much!

April Tsang (9)
Estcourt Preparatory School

Mr Nobody

I know a man who is always dozy,
Who never cleans the floor.
He leaves the garden a typical mess,
He'll be dozy for evermore.
Though he leaves dirty fingerprints everywhere,
Everybody knows it was . . . Mr Nobody.

He puts damp wood upon the fire,
Kettles never boil in Nobody's house.
The mud comes in from Nobody's shoes,
Nobody comes in Mr Nobody's house . . .
Because of the mouse.
The things he buys are always lost,
Nobody tosses them about
But Mr Nobody.

Emma Stewart (10)
Estcourt Preparatory School

Equine Mania

Weekend's here, my favourite thing I now pursue,
Which is not going to the nearest zoo,
But is going to my local stable,
Riding Pinky, Spring or Mable.

Monday to Friday seven o'clock, my alarm bell goes,
Rising for school is hard you knows,
Saturday morning seven o'clock, my alarm bell rings,
Where am I? Up, dressed, in my riding things.

Unusual items stuffed in my pockets, I force,
For brushing, combing and tit bits of course,
A carrot, Polo mint, sugar lumps and apple,
For good behaviour or for the new grey dapple.

I love to ride, trot, canter and hack,
Over the jumps or around the track,
On a Welsh mountain, conamara or cob,
The fun's the same on Henry, Rupert or Bob.

As I travel on and on without a rest,
My heart beats quickly in my chest,
Up and over the jumps on a bay Exmoor,
Or performing dressage for a higher score.

The thrill of being on a pony's back,
Cleaning and polishing his leather tack,
This is the life for me,
Why can't my parents see?

It's not the school work I want to do,
It's riding Connie, Holly or Zanadoo.

Jessica Greenwood (9)
Estcourt Preparatory School

Sweets

Lots of sweets stored in jars,
Delicious things like candy bars.

Strawberry creams and chocolate mice,
Both of them are very nice.

Cones filled high with soft ice cream,
Extra toppings, what a dream.

Cola bottles, sherbet dips,
Haribo and cherry lips.

Dairy Milk and Cadbury's Flake,
Icing on my birthday cake.

Multicoloured rainbow drops,
Toffee apples, lollipops.

I don't know what my mum will say,
When she finds out I've tooth decay!

Sarah Bates (11)
Estcourt Preparatory School

Some Good Friends

There is this girl called Olivia,
She loves to play Disney trivia.

She has a best friend called Natasha,
For short, people call her Basha.

Grace is a lovely girl,
She just has a few blonde curls.

Olivia has a pen pal called Lidia,
She has a friend called Dona Didia.

Lucy is soon to be eleven,
But her sister is only seven.

As you probably already know,
These friends can put on a terrific show.

Olivia Torr (10)
Estcourt Preparatory School

When I Went Shopping

On the last day of September,
I started to remember
All the times, having fun,
Shopping with my mum.

We looked in all the shops,
Until we found some tops,
My mum turned round and said to me,
'Come on, let's have some tea.'

After tea she said to me,
'What would you like to be?'
I answered her with great respect,
'I think I'd like to be a vet!'

In the car coming home,
We spoke to Dad on the phone,
He told us he'd been working hard,
We said, 'We've used up your credit card!'

Hearing this he blew a fuse,
He didn't want to hear this news,
We looked around, didn't dare to speak,
Or tell him that we're going back next week!

Rebecca Rooney (10)
Estcourt Preparatory School

Dolphins In Danger

Dolphins playing happily beneath the deep blue sea,
Dolphins playing happily, happy as can be.
Along comes a big black boat puffing out smoke,
Tipping pollution into the sea which makes dolphins choke.
They die of this pollution and float to the top,
Along comes a fishing boat and collects them in the nets they drop.
The fishermen were astonished that they
And their poison could have caused this misery.
They called the WDCS and told them the problem
And they said, 'You must stop pollution now!'

Ashleigh Cruse (9)
Estcourt Preparatory School

Conker

On a crisp autumn day deep in a wood,
There hung a conker shell blowing like it should.

As the wind raged, it shook the conker shell down
And it fell softly to the cold, muddy ground.

There lay the opened shell, hidden by a carpet of leaves,
It rested there for a couple of weeks and its only company
was a few prickly weeds.

Autumn passed and winter too and from the ground the conker grew,
First the roots, then the shoot, followed by leaves that made it cute.

Years passed by, the sapling changed, its twiggy stem
does not remain,
Instead there stands a strong fine tree with conkers hanging
for you and me.

Morgan Prescott (10)
Estcourt Preparatory School

There Is No Place Like Home

When you're feeling sad or alone,
There's no place like home.
When you feel blue but don't want to moan,
There's no place like home.
When you need somebody to talk to but don't have a phone,
There's no place like home.
When you talk to your friends but they use the wrong tone,
There's no place like home.
When you need to let out your feelings, break the comb,
There's no place like home.
When you're not feeling well and just want to groan,
There's no place like home.

Now we know that home is special to us,
Let's keep it that way and not make a fuss.

Rea Patel (10)
Estcourt Preparatory School

Charles Jenkins

Ben, Sam, William and me,
Four cousins are we,
Each love drawing, painting thoroughly,
Perhaps it runs in the family?

My grandpa always loved to paint,
The world he saw as pictures,
A secret creature in every painting,
A ladybird to find!

Ben, Sam, William and me,
We would just love to see our grandpa,
But we cannot because
He has passed away so terribly.

Colourful, sensational drawings,
Paintings really inspiring to see,
All I know of Grandpa now is . . .
How truly loved he will always be.

Heather Lacey (10)
Estcourt Preparatory School

My Wonderful Elephant

My elephant thinks I'm wonderful,
My elephant thinks I'm cool,
My elephant hangs around with me
And follows me to school,
My elephant likes the way I look,
He thinks that I am fun and smart,
He thinks that I am kind and generous
And have a terrific heart,
My elephant thinks I'm brave and bold,
He's proud of my strength and guts,
But mostly he likes the way I smell,
My elephant thinks I'm nuts.

Sahrish Qasim (10)
Estcourt Preparatory School

The Blue Guinea Pig

I'm the blue guinea pig,
Not like any other,
I'm not very big,
But neither is my mother.

I'm the blue guinea pig,
Striped, spotted and cute,
I really like to dig
And pull up all the roots.

Small, round and fat,
Not like any other,
I descended from a bat,
Or maybe from an otter.

I have a brown wig,
So people don't freak out,
I'm not very big
And some say I have a snout.

I like to play with glue
And stick things on my brother,
But he doesn't have a clue it's me
And neither does my mother.

I'm the blue guinea pig,
Not like any other,
I'm not very big,
But neither is my mother.

Alexandra Nield (9)
Estcourt Preparatory School

The Park

One day I was walking in the park,
With my mate, Marc,
It was autumn time,
So I wrote you this rhyme.
I ran though the park,
I made a dog bark,
There was different coloured leaves,
So I said them in Japanese,
There was brown and orange leaves,
Red and yellow leaves.
A toddler was throwing them in the air,
As I was watching the leaves in the air,
I noticed a robin redbreast,
With her baby robins in her nest.
Then I sat down on a nearby bench,
It started raining and I got drenched,
That was just my luck,
But then I saw a tiny duck,
It didn't stop raining, but then the sun came out,
All of a sudden a rainbow came out!

Lucy Bradley (10)
Estcourt Preparatory School

What If?

What if I was a mermaid?
What if a crab was yellow and green striped?
What if catfish had square heads?
What if whales swam on their backs?
And what if sharks ate so many fish there were none left?

What if the sun was made out of tiny pieces of sherbet lemons?
What if golf was played with a hockey stick?
What if football was played with a rugby ball?
What if at swimming you wore a tracksuit to swim in?
And what if netball was played with a boomerang?

Danielle Wildbore (9)
Estcourt Preparatory School

Toy Cat In The River

We decided to go to the park,
After we had had our dinner,
We walked across the stepping stones
And Jasmine's cat fell in the river.

It went sailing down the river like a boat,
It was the funniest thing I'd seen,
Dad began to shout,
Jasmine began to scream.

So Dad took off his shoes and socks,
He is very bold,
He waded through the water
And said it was very cold.

Dad held onto a branch that hung from a tree,
He was getting very wet,
Jasmine was still screaming
As Dad stretched for her pet.

Dad managed to get the cat,
That had been stuck on a rock in the river,
Jasmine stopped her screaming
And Dad began to shiver.

Natalie Newton (10)
Estcourt Preparatory School

The Pop Idol Pony

There was a young pony called Bridle
Who decided to enter Pop Idol,
He sang like a dream
And was only sixteen,
So he went right through to the final!

Charlotte Tilley (10)
Estcourt Preparatory School

Scuba-Diving

I put on my wetsuit, so hard to do,
Snorkel, mask and flippers too.
The air tank is strapped to my back,
With a regulator to breathe with and no time to flap.
I waddle to the water, frightened but excited.

Swimming out to sea,
Testing the buoyancy.
Floating on the top,
Sinking to the bottom.
Underwater pressure makes me feel as light as a feather.
I want to stay here forever.

Forefinger to thumb meaning OK,
Thumb up to emerge,
Thumb down to descend,
Wobbly hand for ear problem.

The fish are colourful and happy to be near me,
When I tap on a rock they come over to see.

I'm all out of air, from breathing too fast,
I must come up, it will not last.

When I come from the sea, the weights pull me down,
I fall to my feet and collapse to the ground.

Emma Taylor (10)
Estcourt Preparatory School

You Won't Believe This!

As I opened the creaking door,
Spiders and cobwebs along the floor,
I stepped into the haunted house,
I heard a noise, was it a bat, cat or even a mouse?

I slowly walked into the opposite room,
I saw a witch on a wooden broom,
With a pointed hat and crooked teeth
And a cauldron with a black cat underneath!

I tried to stay calm and be as brave as I could,
Shaking and quivering but bravely I stood,
Walking on further along the dark hall,
Not knowing what was ahead of me as I stood so tall!

It was all pitch-black, I didn't know where to go,
Left or right, to or fro,
There up beside me was a bright flashing light,
Going towards it I knew it was right.

I ran and ran as fast as I could,
Out through the door and into the woods,
I jumped and gave myself a scare,
You won't believe this, it was a nightmare!

Lauren Lockett (10)
Estcourt Preparatory School

The Sleepover

At my sleepover we play and play,
All sorts of games throughout the day.
As the hours go by into the night,
The time has come for a pillow fight.

A midnight feast is always nice,
With fizzy drinks and chocolate mice.
Telling stories about scary ghosts,
The creepy ones we like the most.

It's getting late, we're feeling sleepy,
We hear strange noises, it seems so creepy.
One by one we look out the door,
It's my little sister on the floor.

We climb into bed, we're tired of play,
It's been a long and busy day.
We close our eyes and no one peeps
And in two minutes time, we're fast asleep.

Natalie Agarwal (9)
Estcourt Preparatory School

My Favourite Teddy

My favourite teddy is cute and cuddly,
I never take him in the bath because
It's too bubbly.
He is the colour brown
And I bought him from the town.
His name is Trigger
And his best friend is Tigger.
They play together every day,
They go to the park, day after day
And never forget the way.
My favourite teddy I will never forget,
Even if I get a pet.

Gabrielle Rhodes (10)
Estcourt Preparatory School

A Day At The Zoo

The elephant was the first animal we saw,
It was grey, big and fat,
Wandering round its muddy pen,
Looking for its hat.

We heard the lions roaring
And saw them tearing meat,
It was a terrifying sight,
I am glad it's not my feet.

When I was walking with my friend,
I heard a little noise,
I looked around and there I saw,
Some ducklings chased by boys.

Next we saw some tall giraffes
And little baby ones,
Their necks were really very long,
Touching flying swans.

Ten big monkeys going crazy,
Swinging from tree to tree,
Some were eating ripe bananas,
For their lovely tea.

The last thing we did in the zoo
Was to go in the fountain shop,
I was going to buy a teddy bear,
But instead I bought a top.

Helen Gourley (9)
Estcourt Preparatory School

Shopping

Shopping, shopping in Oldham Town
Going on escalators, up and down
Looking at T-shirts, jeans, ponchos and skirts
When I've spent my money, it really hurts

I go in lots of shops
Bay Trading and Next
If I had to choose
It would have to be IDX

Then last but not least the sweet shop
I go to choose my sweets
Yum-yum
Thornton's here I come

Then I go home
Put on my clothes
Look in the mirror
And off to Mario's.

Georgia Hicks (9)
Estcourt Preparatory School

Luzley End Farm

L iving in Luzley,
U nderstanding the country,
Z oo-like, with animals,
L oving the life,
E veryone is friendly,
Y ou really feel like you belong.

E very day you learn something new,
N ight-time still and quiet,
D aytime is busy with skies of blue.

F orever I would like to stay,
A lways on this farm,
R ainy or sunny,
M y lovely Luzley End Farm.

Grace Holland (10)
Estcourt Preparatory School

My Cousins

My cousins are called Mia, Lola and Helena,
Lola is 1 year old,
Helena is 11 months.

Helena has a big sister called Mia,
She is 3 years old
And the best 3-year-old friend anyone could have!

Mia started walking about 2 years ago,
Lola has been for about 2 weeks,
But Helena has just started learning!

Lola can say 'ducky',
Helena says 'hello' and 'hiya'
And Mia's first word was 'Poppy'!

Helena,
Mia
And Lola are all the best.

I love them,
I hope they love me too!

Poppy Robinson (9)
Estcourt Preparatory School

My Best Friends

B hakti is very bright,
E mily is always right.
S hardha is really kind,
T anya has a great mind.

F iona is really nice,
R achael has beautiful eyes.
I sabel is quite smart,
E mma has a big, kind heart.
N atalie is good at art.
D anielle truly loves her bunny,
S ophie is really funny.

Laura Ferns (10)
Estcourt Preparatory School

A Poem About My Dog

My dog is called Casey
And he has a habit that's crazy.
He likes to watch TV,
As he lies on the floor next to me.
His favourite snack is cheese strings,
He loves to eat them in the evenings.
He likes to play with his ball
And tries to bite the postman when he calls.
My friend and I take him to the park,
Where he runs around and barks.
He tried to catch a cat one day
And dragged me all the way.
Mum brings him to school in the morning
And comes back with him in the evening.
I love my dog so much
And he's cuter than the dog next door called Butch.

Danielle Riley (10)
Estcourt Preparatory School

My Dream Animal

My dream animal would have . . .
The tail of a bunny,
The purr of a cat,
It wouldn't cost money,
It would wear a hat,
The eyes of a dog,
It could see through the fog,
The fur of a bear,
If you needed a friend it would always be there,
The trot of a horse,
It would run your cross-country course,
The beak of a parrot,
It eats healthy carrots,
It wouldn't need walking, riding or brushing,
Just a cuddle from you would do fine!

Olivia Ketley (10)
Estcourt Preparatory School

Bubbles

Bubbles is my special friend,
I love him lots and lots.
I can speak to Bubbles,
But he can't talk back.

Bubbles has bright yellow eyes
And a nose that's pink and wet.
He has ears as black as coal
And paws as white as snow.

His whiskers are long and thin
And his ears are small and fluffy.
He has fur as smooth as silk
And a tail that's soft as well.

Bubbles climbs up trees
And even climbs on roofs.
He runs after squirrels
And chases birds away.

Bubbles likes his fish,
He also likes his milk.
But I'm not too sure about his water,
As he splashes this about!

Have you guessed who my special friend is yet?
Well, I will tell you.
He is, of course,
My lovely black and white cat.

Rachael Bolton (9)
Estcourt Preparatory School

Autumn

Autumn is the best time of the year,
Because we know that Christmas is near,
But before that there is Hallowe'en and Bonfire Night
And plenty of things that give us a fright.

At Hallowe'en, children go trick or treating,
With pumpkin lanterns to light their meetings,
People sit in the dark, telling scary tales,
It gives people a fright and they wake hearing wails.

Bonfire Night is colourful and exciting,
The fireworks brighten the sky like lightning,
We eat toffee apples around the bonfire,
As the flames rise up, higher and higher.

In autumn all the leaves fall off the trees
And swirl around in the breeze,
The colours of the leaves are red, orange, brown and gold,
In autumn the weather can be hot or cold.

The days get shorter and the nights are long,
But the birds are gone so you can't hear their song,
We watch squirrels collecting acorns,
All wrapped in our scarves and hats, nice and warm.

Emma Sibson (10)
Estcourt Preparatory School

Seasons

Spring is around once again,
Where flowers start to grow again,
Baby animals are being born inside,
Whilst the rain showers the fields outside.

The summer sun shines through the sky,
As the girls and boys fly their kites way up high,
The melting ice cream in our hands,
As our feet are buried deep in the sand.

Autumn comes but once a year,
Showing us that Jack Frost is very near,
Golden glows of bonfires afar,
Showering the earth with shiny sparks.

The cold winds of winter are finally here,
With falling snow landing on our ears,
The Christmas trees with flashing lights,
Shows the way through the wintry nights.

The four different seasons come nicely together,
To give us lots of different weather,
From the rain and sun that makes flowers grow,
To the wind and snow that makes them go.

Mariam Ahmed (9)
Estcourt Preparatory School

What A Shop

As I walked down my street
I heard a squeak
What do you think I saw?

A noisy pet shop,
A squeaking, chirping pet shop,
A lively pet shop,
A splashing, dashing pet shop.

There were . . .
Tiny gerbils,
Furry hamsters,
Purring cats,
Thank you, no bats!

The cute little puppies,
Were next to the bunnies.
But, the parrots that speak
Were asleep.

At least the fish were quiet,
As they swam tirelessly around.
From them I could barely hear a sound.

As I walked down my street,
I passed the pet shop by,
I tripped on the pavement,
Ooh, what a squeak,
Then I was on the floor.

Bianca Crisci (10)
Estcourt Preparatory School

The End Of The Rainbow

There's a rainbow here,
Let's go near,
For we have been told,
There might be a pot of gold,
At the end of the rainbow.

There are Irish legends
About leprechaun fellows,
For we have been told
They guard the pot of gold
At the end of the rainbow.

As we get near,
We start to hear
A little noise,
It sounds like a voice,
It must be the leprechaun.

But as we got there,
We cried in despair,
For the rainbow had gone
And so had the leprechaun.

But as we looked down,
Down to the ground,
To our delight, shiny and bright,
Two gold coins,
Bathed in colourful light,
From the end of the rainbow.

Sophie Smith (9)
Estcourt Preparatory School

The Four Seasons

In spring flowers start to bloom,
Sheep will have lambs soon,
Trees start to form leaves,
There is also a light breeze.

In summer the skies are blue,
The sun shines all day through,
Picnics by the sea,
Strawberries and cream for my tea.

In autumn trees turn from green to gold,
Their leaves are bright and bold,
Catherine wheels and fireworks explode in the night,
Hallowe'en gives people a fright.

In winter it turns frosty and cold,
Christmas colours are warm and bold,
Santa Claus is making a list,
My stocking is full of wonderful gifts.

Chloe Shaw (10)
Estcourt Preparatory School

All Weather

W eather changes all year round.
E ach season is different, the clouds move around.
A ll through spring it is wet and damp,
    not much fun when going to camp.
T he summer is full of sun,
    it's the time for paddling pools and having fun.
H ere is autumn, fresh and crisp, in the mornings there may be mist,
    leaves on trees turn red and gold, playing in the park,
    wrapped up from the cold.
E ventually it is winter with ice and snow,
    snuggling by the fire, keeping warm in the glow.
R ain and sunshine, snow and ice,
    the clouds move around to make the weather nice.

Lauren Cunliffe (10)
Estcourt Preparatory School

I Want To Be Grown Up

I want to wear high heels
And beautiful bright red lipstick,
Lots of sparkling diamonds,
I'd be a real hot chick.

I want to paint my nails
And party all night long,
Go on the karaoke
And sing my favourite song.

I want to go out shopping,
In all the trendy places,
Buy lots of fancy clothes
And see lots of famous faces.

I'd like a fast sports car
And travel to my friend's,
We could go out driving,
From John O'Groats to Land's End.

I want to work in an office,
With views overlooking the sea
And I'd make loads of money
And drink lots of tea.

I want a big old house,
With lions at the gate
And my very own bedroom,
I could leave in an awful state.

The problem with my plan,
Although it may seem fine,
Is I won't be able to do it
Because I'm only nine!

Eleanor Wild (9)
Estcourt Preparatory School

If I Were . . .

If I were a dog
I would bark all day,
But I am not, I would say.
If I were a dog,
I would dream to be stroked,
But I am not.

If I were a cat
I would pounce all day,
But I am not, I would say.
If I were a cat,
I would love to jump high,
'It's not true . . .' I would cry.

If I were a bird
I would fly all day,
But I am not, I would say.
If I were a bird,
I would sit on the tree, off the ground,
'I can't,' I said with a frown.

If I were a mouse
I would run around all day,
But I am not, I would say.
But I am just
Plain, old . . . *me!*

Shradha Amin (9)
Estcourt Preparatory School

Kiss

If you kiss a bush,
Don't be in a rush.

If you kiss a fence,
You'll get one pence.

If you kiss a flower,
You get more power.

If you kiss the grass,
You think of the past.

If you kiss leaves,
You'll get a pod of peas.

If you kiss a stone,
You'll get a phone.

If you kiss a tree,
You'll get stung by a bee.

If you kiss water,
You'll get a daughter.

If you kiss a weed,
You'll do a good deed.

Lucy Crossland (9)
Estcourt Preparatory School

Animals In The World

Horses can come from all around the world,
Dogs with straight tails and some are curled,
Monkeys are such amazing creatures,
Elephants have such unusual features,
Lions, the king of the jungle, what beasts,
Tigers that hunt for lots of meats,
Parrots are animals which can talk,
Penguins have a very strange walk,
Turtles are fast and very sweet,
Pigs could never stay nice and neat,
Sharks have very sharp teeth,
Dolphins which stay in the sea beneath,
Sheep, their wool so cosy and warm,
Chicks that live and stay on the farm,
Fish like water that is deep,
Crocodiles as pets you could not keep,
Rabbits jump around and around,
Snakes that slither along the ground,
Zebras that resemble a pelican crossing,
Camels with bad breath need to start flossing,
There's too many animals, they're making me dizzy,
No wonder the world feels so busy!

Gemma Green (10)
Estcourt Preparatory School

I Wish

Last night as I lay in my bed,
I looked up to the sky and I said,
'I wish I could be an astronaut!'

To hop and jump just like a kanga,
Or maybe just like an oranga.

I would have a fab night,
Whizzing and whirling just like a kite.

I'd give each star a special name,
So they all wouldn't seem the same.

I think each star would sparkle and tinkle,
Gold dust on each to make them twinkle.

I'd gather a few little ones to take home,
So I wouldn't feel quite so alone.

An astronaut would have such fun,
Way up high, away from the sun.

The moon would be a glorious venture,
Jewels and goodies to pick for adventure.

My rocket would be of silver and red,
Oh it's just like my bed!

Brittany Ashworth (10)
Estcourt Preparatory School

What I Found One Day

One day I found,
A glistening mirror on the ground.
A large white blanket so fluffy and light
And a giant, round, white visitor
Who had come to stay the night.
A piece of black paper covered with glitter
Was stapled to the sky!
And I found a hooting creature that began to cry.
Mud and water that covered the kitchen floors
And lovely hot toast when I came indoors.
Hot marshmallows all toasted and nice
And hundreds of candles that smelt of rich spice.
Creamy hot chocolate that I desire
And a book to read by the crackling fire.
Furry slippers and a lovely warm gown,
Some delicious cakes all golden-brown.
A little red bird in the corner of the shed
And a hot-water bottle in my very large bed.
Now, in my bed, I will dream,
What do these things mean to me?

Zarah Amin (10)
Estcourt Preparatory School

I Love Tennis

Tennis is a smashing sport,
It's great running on the court,
When the ball comes near my racket,
I get into position and whack it,
My tennis coach told me to put top spin on the ball,
But it didn't work and went flying into the wall.
There we go, finished the game,
It wasn't bad but my back is in pain.

Bethany Ross (9)
Estcourt Preparatory School

Hallowe'en

Witches and wizards cast their spells,
Which frighten the bishop of Bath and Wells,
In their cauldrons frogs' legs, bats' wings
And lots of other scary things.

Ghosts and ghouls scour the streets,
In search of trick or treats.
Pumpkins carved, candles lit,
We all feel scared, well just a bit!

Scary sounds like creaky bones,
Dark shadows and muffled moans,
Slowly sneaking to find what's there,
Relieved, it's just the cat on the chair.

My friends arrive, a scary crowd,
Fangs and blood and howls so loud.
We join the others going door to door,
Treacle toffee we get and lots, lots more.

Bobbing apples and games all done,
My friends all go, one by one.
I'm tired and weary, legs like lead,
Slowly upstairs, I'm off to bed.

Georgina Bennett (10)
Estcourt Preparatory School

Asleep

Fluffy and round
Not making a sound
Pup lies asleep in his pen

Head on paws
Not a sign of his claws
Tail lying flat on the ground

Little black nose
And soft floppy ears
Twitching when someone comes near

Tranquil and quiet
With no sign of riot
Our puppy sleeps peaceful and content

Without any warning
Little puppy starts yawning
Pawing the sleep from his eyes

Tail madly wagging
Ears pricked up in the air
Bounding and leaping, pup's no longer sleeping.

Gabrielle Norcross (9)
Estcourt Preparatory School

The Wind Is Like . . .

The wind is like a swan gliding softly through the air,
It rustles the trees and sweeps you away,
Whistling, whistling for evermore.

The wind is like a young beaver paddling in the ocean,
It goes over the wide sea and sweeps you away,
Rushing, rushing for evermore.

The wind is like a dolphin riding on the waves,
It jumps over the clouds and sweeps you away,
Riding, riding for evermore.

Jessica Fern Draper (9)
Halsall CE Primary School

A Very Blustery Day

It was a very blustery day,
The wind ran quickly through my hair like a cold hairdryer,
It tugged at my coat like my baby brother,
The grey clouds moved aggressively across the sky,
Like my sister on a bad day!
The wind made the old oak tree seem very polite by waving at me,
The trees rustled and danced until the wind calmed down.

Melissa Schofield (10)
Halsall CE Primary School

On A Windy Autumn Morning

On a windy autumn morning
With the wind as cold as an ice block
When the trees rustle and sneeze
And I feel the wind breathing on my face.

I hear the wind whistling in my ear sharing its secrets
I feel the wind tugging me along like a game of tug of war
I can see the wind dancing, teasing the leaves in the cold breeze.

Tom Barlow (10)
Halsall CE Primary School

The Windy Playground

Trees whispering like people talking to each other
The smell of clean, fresh, cut grass billowing around people's coats
The wind brushing my hair in all directions like magnetic forces
Cars rushing like arrows darting through the wind
Leaves gushing in my face like a giant hairdryer
It sweeps you away into a world of your own
The trees look like dancers performing the Nutcracker.

Holly Bartlett (9)
Halsall CE Primary School

A Windy Morning

On a wet and windy morning,
Trees rustling in the air,
Creaking and crackling.

The taste of the cold, frosty morning,
Blowing on my tongue,
The sun dazzles through the clouds
And hurts my eyes.

The cold wind blowing in my face,
Making my hair stand up,
People hugging their coats as they walk along.

The morning smells of fresh manure,
Being pushed across the playground,
By the mischievous wind.

Edward Webster (10)
Halsall CE Primary School

Wind Blow On Me

Clean fresh air rushing down my mouth
Like a boat sailing down a stream.

The strong wind knotting my hair
Like I have just woken up.

Children screaming while the trees
Whisper to one another.

Trees dancing like there is a
Great party in the sky.

The wind guiding itself around me
As the leaves float gently to the hard tarmac ground.

Jennifer Kitching (9)
Halsall CE Primary School

On A Windy Autumn Morning

On a windy autumn morning,
When the wind is fresh and chilled,
Where the trees rustle and sneeze
And the leaves dance on the cool breeze.

On a fresh autumn morning,
When the wind whistles through my hair,
Where the wind freezes my cold hands
And the taste of the fresh cool air.

The wind is as wintry as an ice block,
That makes the trees swish and sway,
It blows everyone who dares to go out,
On a windy autumn day!

Laura Wilkinson (10)
Halsall CE Primary School

My Five Senses

My five senses sense the wind
Howling over the playground,
Like a fierce wolf
And the sky is a smoky grey.

The air smelt dewy all around me,
Like I'm in a swimming pool.

The clouds moved across the sky
As fast as a Ferrari on a smooth racetrack.

Thomas Greenwood (10)
Halsall CE Primary School

Wind

You can hear the mighty wind howling
Through the old trees.
You can feel a cold force pushing,
Pushing you along.

You can see trees bending
Like a giant hand is pushing them.
You can hear the trees whistling
Sharing their secrets.

James Caffery (9)
Halsall CE Primary School

The Haunted House

The crashed door swayed nervously,
Stone cracking tiles shrieked disturbingly,
I shuffled on,
At the stairs, silky cobwebs dangled around me
And the splintered wooden stairs collapsed as I touched them.

There was a carpet of broken glass;
Ripped, bloodstained curtains were sprawled over the furniture.
I held my breath . . .
For a closet fell next to me with a skeleton in it!

A chilly breeze sent me shivering like ice.
A cold, white, ghostly figure swooped towards me.
It carried a pointed object,
But its piercing cackle made me forget.
I closed my eyes
And a sharp pain rang through my stomach . . .
I knew I was dead.

Katherine Mair (10)
Highfield Priory School

The Haunted Manor Whispers To Me

I stare as the eyes stare back at me,
A shiver goes down my spine as I realise,
My legs go over to the blackened hollow,
Under the door, with my body keen to follow
And I'm sure,
Beneath the ivy-poisoned I know,
Through the door, I need to go,
I stand in the hallway, frozen with fear,
And I understand - the thing is near.

Up the stairs, through the hall,
My hand is shaking on the wall.
I am getting closer,
Running along, I am blinded by cobwebs,
Made heavier by the gathering dust.
Nerves hold me back, but go on I must.
Nearly there, I opened the door, entered the room
And out of the window, saw a blue moon
And I guessed that somewhere a werewolf howled.

The time is near, the time is right,
For the death-day of the manor is tonight.
I shall not be scared, but in a whisper,
I am going to fight, but in a whisper . . .

In a whisper, I am going to die!

Eleanor Newton (10)
Highfield Priory School

The Haunted House

It was a cold, dark night,
That made me shiver like a snowman,
I tiptoed past the lion head watching over me.
The silence of the pitch-black as I entered
The eerie place everyone is scared of,
I had to,
I had to prove that I wasn't scared.

The floorboards creaked as I scurried to a lamp.
I crept up the stairs,
Watching everywhere, shaking in fear.
Watching to see if a ghost creeps up behind
And takes me away . . .
I finally made it up the stairs,
But the door creaked open.

Someone was in there, but who?
I tried to get out but the run to the door
Seemed to go on forever . . .
I finally made it,
It was too late,
Something turned around,
But it was only my friend.

Alice Kelly (11)
Highfield Priory School

Spirits Of The Mansion

I scurried past the rotting walls
The sweat dripping
Heavily from my brow
The front door
Infested with woodlice
Shrieked as I pulled
Banging behind me

I ventured onward
Up the flimsy
Treacherous stairs
Beats pounding my chest
Through my ribs
Spirits swirling
Gracefully in the air

Eerie sounds from the wall
A burst of
Light!
Swoosh!
Through me went a
Ghost with big shackles
Clanging in the air
All sense was lost!

Kieran Jandu (10)
Highfield Priory School

The Haunted House

As I walk past the haunted house
In the dead of night,
The driveway groans as I gallop on,
All the time the spirits are haunting me,
I push the door and . . . I see the Devil,
I scream to myself and enter.

As I walk, I hear chains clang,
Shackles chase after me,
The stairs wail as I tread,
I shake like a leaf as I stumble onwards,
The floorboards creak, while I slide,
Now I can see the door.

As I scurry on,
The door runs away from me,
I dive and it grabs my ankles.
I suddenly feel myself lurch forward,
I land on the grass then run and run home.

Nathan White (10)
Highfield Priory School

Haunted House

The night before Hallowe'en
Was treacherous
I kept waking up
I crept downstairs for a drink of cold water

As I did so
I heard the ghosts and spirits waking
I heard them coming towards me
They were coming closer and closer and closer

I stormed back upstairs
But tiptoed past Dad's room
I could still hear him snoring
Phew - I was safe!

Xanthe Graham-Waring (10)
Highfield Priory School

The Haunted House

Grandma looks old
Grandma is old
House looks old
House is very old

The roof is as sharp as a knife
The chimney is dusty
The walls bulged
The house was strange

The door crept towards me
The floorboards groaned
The wind howled
The windows rattled

The house was a nightmare
The ghouls growled
Spiders crawled all around
And it was the *haunted house.*

George Huck (10)
Highfield Priory School

Haunted House

I went to a haunted house
And what did I see?
Some flying plates
And locking gates.

I went to a haunted house
And what did I hear?
Some howls out loud
And screams so clear.

I went to a haunted house
And what did I see?
I trembled with fright
And ran with all my might.

Grace Mitchell (10)
Highfield Priory School

The Haunted House

It was an ice-cold moonlit night,
As I crept along the bendy roads.
I looked up and saw a massive house,
I was so pleased,
After three hours of tiring steps I had arrived.

The door moved away from me,
I was surrounded by empty black coffins,
I was terrified!
Spiderwebs hung from the ceiling,
Like curtains that had been hung there
For hundreds of years.

It was as black as a coal mine,
I tiptoed up the creaky stairs,
There were four rooms upstairs,
I crept into the final room, the wind whistled,
A wardrobe door opened, a ghost appeared!
It started to chase me, I ran down the stairs.

The ghost didn't give up easily,
I ran for an hour with the ghost behind me,
I stopped and collapsed,
I had given up,
I pinched myself and woke up,
Phew! No ghosts could get me now,
I was safe.

Olivia Carter (10)
Highfield Priory School

The Haunted House

I dashed to next door,
But the clock struck 12,
I was too late,
I crept into the house.
The door was creaking,
I stepped back a pace or two,
I fell down a slippery slide,
I couldn't believe my eyes.

I fell into a ghost train,
The seats were soft as a dove,
This was a ridiculous thing,
The ride stopped.
There was the picture of Black Tom's tomb,
The picture moved towards me.
This is a familiar thing I thought,
I jumped out of the way.

Then this ghost walked towards me,
It was a girl ghost,
She was murmuring.
Then she fainted away,
Suddenly I was chained up.
There was a spell book in front of me,
I read it out loud,
I was back home in my bed.

Devika Tadi (10)
Highfield Priory School

The Haunted House

The rain was plunging down on the road,
As I sneaked to the door of the haunted house.
It creaked open,
I screamed,
I scampered up the hall.
I hid in the compact chest.
I heard screams and shouts.

Out of the box I crept,
Then *crash, bang, wallop!*
A skeleton fell from the roof.
I dashed into a room,
But then . . . *snatch!* It took me from behind
And down the black hole I went.

Everything was silent . . .
Dark and cold.
I just kept howling,
But it didn't help.
Death just passed me by.

Oliver Parker (10)
Highfield Priory School

Strolling Through The Cemetery

Zombies lurched through the cemetery of rotting carcasses,
The child accelerated in the dim moonlight,
Rapidly he sprinted,
In and out of the tombs,
Zombies left, right and centre,
The sculptures snigger . . .

He kicked open the rotten, timber door,
It squealed and bellowed, 'Ow!'
The creaking floorboards were trod on,
The mortal remains laid down flat,
It's gory!
He trembled, like shivering children in the frost.

Steadily he sat
On an old, rusty tool box,
The zombies crept nearer,
Hands steadily stretched,
He stood up and pulled a bit of a smile,
He had a stoic-looking expression on his face.

Thomas Wood (10)
Highfield Priory School

The Haunted House

I walked swiftly up to the house in the ice-cold night,
Oh, what a cold night, I felt a shiver in my blood,
The wind howled like a wolf on a moonlit night.
I looked at the house and its creepy windows,
With the billowing curtains looking back at me,
I was afraid!

Then the gate groaned as I pushed past it,
With an eerie feeling I knew I was being watched,
Like an owl watching its prey at night,
I entered the house and felt a paranormal activity,
The chairs rattled and the curtains flapped in the wind,
I dashed into a room, but I didn't hear a comforting noise,
All I heard was the clanking of a chain.

I heard the crack of the door behind me,
Hearing a cold, wheezy laugh,
I feared for my life, I ran, fumbling for my keys,
I had not rescued my brother.

Aidan Panagarry (10)
Highfield Priory School

The Haunted House

Set upon a crumbling high hill
Surrounded by an uninviting graveyard
The haunted house watched me
With decaying eyes
As I galloped past mad Alice's grave
And stood shivering in the eerie, cold wind
Shall I go in?

I grabbed the door handle
The rotten door creaked open
The cobweb-filled passages
Were dark and murky
The wind howled my name . . .
Bats screamed and flew out of the door

I ran back through the broken door
I glanced back and saw
The mysterious house clattering its shutters.

James Smith (10)
Highfield Priory School

Haunted House

The gloomy day became worse
So I scurried past the shattered glass
And . . . and . . . the house was mouldy

It was humid
Statues of goblins
Dust everywhere
I tiptoed upstairs
A vase

Crash

I ran scarcely
Old doors screaming
I went in the attic
The weeping steps groaned in agony
I fumbled, the door howled and . . .
I was locked in
I shrieked, '*Help! Someone.*'
Bats flew out at every angle

I'd seen a window, it wouldn't open
Then I gave up
But a breeze like a hurricane
I looked up, there it was
The passage out
I slid down the roof
My life was cut short . . .
Dead!

Jessica Moore (10)
Highfield Priory School

The Haunted House

As I walked through the woods,
Conkers fell to the ground,
Autumn leaves whispered in the wind
And the darkness, oh the darkness,
Crept around me like a cloak.

I caught a glimpse of a house,
Through the trees, the moonlight reflected off the roof,
I felt drawn to the house
And almost against my will
Found myself standing outside the door.

I felt as cold as ice,
As I knocked on the door,
Suddenly I felt I was not alone,
I ran as frightened as a mouse,
The flickering and murmuring of the TV screens
Gave it away, I was home!

Katherine Donnelly (10)
Highfield Priory School

The Haunted House

As I walked in the haunted house, the clock struck twelve o'clock.
I heard a noise on the stairs, maybe it was a mouse?
The lights were dim and in the shadow I heard a howling sound.
Maybe it was the wind and rain lashing on the windowpane.
I was trembling with fear that much, I didn't stay to look around,
But ran out of the house so quickly, my feet didn't touch the ground.

Olivia Stead (10)
Highfield Priory School

The Haunted House

I stumbled into the moonlit night,
With the wind howling about me,
I was frightened, it was a dark and gloomy evening,
When I came across the haunted house.

I walked slowly down the muddy path,
The light was dim, the house forbidding,
I thought of evil spirits and spooky ghosts,
I wanted to shout and shriek to send them away.

As I entered the house, I heard the sound of chains rattling,
I climbed the creaking stairs,
Moaning sounds were all I could hear, so I turned and ran.

As I reached the bottom of the stairs,
It felt like there were willowy fingers on my shoulders,
It made me wince!
I longed for the night to end!

Out of the house I ran,
The silvery moon guiding me home,
I left the haunted house behind me,
Never to return!

Emma Bunting (10)
Highfield Priory School

The Haunted House

As I stumbled through the eerie graveyard
The trees screamed as if in agony
And reached towards me, trying to pick me up
And hold me in the spider-black night
I carried on up the path to the house
Dragging my reluctant feet
Because I was as willing to meet a ghost
As someone would be to be bitten by a venomous snake

When at the rotting door
The eye of the moon glared down through the evil black clouds
I took a deep breath and hurriedly forced open the monstrous door
Then, all of a sudden, a ghost appeared
In the shape of an evil lizard spirit
Gruesomely dripping in blood

At the sight of this horrific spectacle my eyes bulged
And my skin turned a bone-white
The moon lit up the nightmare scene
And with a blood-curdling scream the unearthly phantom took flight.

Hal Abraham (10)
Highfield Priory School

The Haunted House

I can hear sounds, see dark and gloomy haunting shadows
On a cold winter's eve,
I step upon the gritty path,
Now I can hear skeleton bones clanging against each other,
I race towards the door,
I turn the handle of the enormous door.

I see red eyes staring at me,
Then they slowly fade,
I walk on the groaning floorboards,
I hear voices that are saying, 'Time to die,'
As I run around the ghostly house, they grow louder and louder.

I run, screaming in fear, up the stairs,
Still the voices grow louder, chasing me as I flee.
I get to a door at the top of the staircase,
I open it . . . I turn to look - I die,
With my blood slithering down the stairs like a snake.

James Turner (11)
Highfield Priory School

War

I was listening to the horrible sound,
Bombs falling and hitting the ground.

Bullets flying everywhere,
The Germans didn't even care.

Bodies thrown over the deserted sidewalk,
Wounded soldiers that couldn't talk.

The trenches were only a warning,
This death could send soldiers mourning.

James Laing (9)
Hulme Court Preparatory School

London

On a train to London, going very fast
Sheep and fields passing by, we arrive at last
I'm ever so excited, I know there's lots to see
To Mum and Dad's tired disgust I'm running around with glee

Straight to the hotel, up in the lift
Mum made me unpack I was really miffed
Next stop the underground (fast but boring)
Our first stop was The Palace, outside it was pouring.

Then the London Eye, high in the air,
From the very, very top you can see everywhere,
Half an hour later the journey was complete,
We went to an Italian for something nice to eat.

Next day the History Museum (it wasn't very great)
Then back to the hotel to meet friends who were late
Princess Diana's fountain, picnic in Hyde Park
We paddled in the fountain until it was nearly dark

Sadly before I knew it, it was time to go back!
My bag with souvenirs weighed like a 10 ton sack
We were so exhausted we could've fallen on the floor
At 2am we got home and I sleepwalked through the door.

Jack Mansley (10)
Hulme Court Preparatory School

The Spider

The spider has eight legs
The spider spins a web
It catches flies, *munch, munch, munch*
The spider's had its lunch!
Here comes the bird
It's after the spider
It gets it in its mouth
Bye-bye spider, it goes south!

Ben Campbell (9)
Hulme Court Preparatory School

Alligator

A n alligator
L ives in a
L ittle swamp
I n America
G reat big teeth are used to
A ttack or even kill
T he enemies for food
O r to take for the family
R eady for a sleep now!

James Fisher (8)
Hulme Court Preparatory School

My Cat

My cat is as hairy as a hamburger
Giddy as a dog
Silly as a child
Kind as my mum
Big as an elephant
Loveable as my puppy
Cuter than my hamster
Posh like the queen
Older than my grandma.

Matthew McDonald (9)
Hulme Court Preparatory School

Fish

F ish darting to and fro
I nside a tank of water
S afe from sharks at sea
H ope you like it in there!

Robert Thackeray (9)
Hulme Court Preparatory School

Hambo, My Hamster

He's a him not a her
Despite his fluffy fur
And if you try to stroke him
Be careful not to choke him

If you try to grab him
He might think you're trying to stab him
He'll happily fight you
He'd love to bite you

He once fell out of his wheel
It was no big deal
He was soon up and runnin'
In his wheel and having fun in

Hambo loves his dinner
He doesn't want to get thinner
Hambo gets in a mood
If he doesn't get his food.

George Littler-Hyde (10)
Hulme Court Preparatory School

Winter

Winter's coming
Nights are getting longer
Feel the freezing ice
Light up your fire
Warm your hands
Before building a snowman
Get your coats on
There's a big fog
Snow is falling down
From the sky
Look out for winter!

Nikesh Mistry (9)
Hulme Court Preparatory School

Dolls

I go into a shop
I see dolls everywhere
Dolls, dolls, they have beautiful faces and hair
Oh, she's like a real girl
Laura is her name
And she comes from Spain
Love is in the air
Because she's got golden hair
She gives me quite a scare
Because I'm a boy and I don't like dolls!

James Foy (10)
Hulme Court Preparatory School

The Cat

I wish I had a cat
I would stroke its fur
And give it a pat
And listen to its purr

It would run and
It would play
I would get it a scratching post
And it would catch its prey.

Jake Riley (9)
Hulme Court Preparatory School

Tigers

I like tigers, they like me
I like it when they jump with glee
They're good at climbing
So watch out if you're something in a tree
Or they will have you for tea.

Benjamin Chorlton-Kerans (9)
Hulme Court Preparatory School

Trip

My worst trip ever
Was last year to Spain.
As I ate my meal,
I was sick on the plane.

Halfway there,
Drinks were given out by men,
I tried a bit of my mum's wine
And I was sick again.

Finally we arrived,
Watching the clock tick,
I had a little swim in the pool
Got out and I was sick.

Next day I got up,
Went for a run on the beach.
I'd been so sick so many times,
My mouth tasted like bleach.

This summer I was bored,
Stuck in with Oldham rain,
But even cooped up in the house
Is better than being in Spain.

Luke Butler (10)
Hulme Court Preparatory School

Blackbird

My dad's got a Honda Blackbird,
The colour is shining blue,
He wears cool black leathers,
His speed is a hundred and two.

The wheels look sweet,
Next to his feet,
With the gears and clocks,
My dad's bike rocks.

Jack Lawrence (9)
Hulme Court Preparatory School

The Cricket Match

The innings has just begun,
Then the batsman starts to run.
A speck is flying in the sky,
Wow! Just watch that ball fly.

Oh no! He's been caught out,
No he's not, the ball's bouncing about.
First he was dropped, then bowled out,
All the other team are jumping about.

At least here comes our best batter,
Silence! There must be no chatter.
Finally! With one more run,
Champions! The test is won.

Sammi Chekroud (9)
Hulme Court Preparatory School

The Weather War

Winter fires huge snowballs,
It also makes a knife of rain.
Winter stabs Spring with it,
Spring must be in pain.

Winter starts up a blizzard,
Spring fires back with the sun.
Winter strikes with thunder and lightning,
This is getting quite fun.

Spring fires lots of leaves,
I think Winter has gone.
Spring finishes Winter off with grass,
Spring has finally won.

Daniel Fielding (9)
Hulme Court Preparatory School

The Alien

Once I saw an alien
He crashed right through the roof
He messed with Jenny's make-up
Then disappeared with a *poof!*

The next time that I saw him
It was quite late at night
It was funny, my friend was there
It gave him quite a fright!

I went to the park one morning
And there he was again
Acting quite peculiar
They put him in a pen

He's still there today
In his alien zoo
I feel quite sorry for him
But I don't know what to do

I s'pose if he's unhappy
He'll disappear again
Leave the zoo in another *poof!*
What will they think then?

Robert Smillie (10)
Hulme Court Preparatory School

The Ruler

Julius Caesar he was a ruler
Did he look tall?
Did it make him cooler?
He lived in Rome
Near the coliseum dome
But how could he move?
He's just a ruler!

Calvin Wong (9)
Hulme Court Preparatory School

Colours Through Another's Eyes

I asked my grandad as he lay on his bed,
'What is colour like?'
'Why green,' he said,
'is like the fresh grass blowing in the wind.'
'Purple,' he sighed,
'is like a thunderstorm raging through the night.'
'Blue,' he thought,
'is like the ocean whose wonders we hardly see.'
'Pink,' he told me,
'is like your bare feet pressing against cold, smooth marble.'
'Orange and yellow,' he explained to me,
'are like wild fires spreading at enormous speeds.'
'And crimson,' he whispered,
'is like the blood of a wounded soldier shot down in a fight . . .'

Akshay Gulati (9)
Hulme Court Preparatory School

I Wish . . .

I wish that all the wars would stop
And we were all happy with glee
There would be no guns, no bombs, no pain
That makes this world seem so insane

I wish there was no hunger
And people didn't starve
That all the world could all be friends
And life could start as new
But I know that this won't happen
Because wishes don't come true.

Joseph Furness (9)
Hulme Court Preparatory School

My New Pup

My puppy is so new,
Cute and cuddly too.
He jumps and he bounds,
In the air and on the ground.

My puppy chases the ball,
He comes whenever you call.
He loves us and he greets us,
He always comes and meets us.

My puppy can be cheeky,
But looks at us so sweetly.
He walks out so proud
And stands out in a crowd.

My puppy can bark so loud,
The post can never be found.
He is my best friend,
I will love him to the end.

Joshua Williams (10)
Hulme Court Preparatory School

Supermarket

Take a trolley, push it around.
Caster sugar? Get a pound.
There's the cocoa, take a tin,
Here's a loaf but it's cut thin.
There's another, that will do,
Now we'll find some jam for you.
Choose a jar. Yes strawberry
Will suit your dad and also me.
A tin of fish, a bag of rice,
That cream-filled cake looks very nice.
We must have soap and toothpaste too,
This green shampoo will do for you.

Rakibul Huda (10)
Hulme Court Preparatory School

Animals

Tigers looking straight at you
Thinking of what they should do
Birds are singing in the tree
Blinking like they're full of glee
Little goldfish in the sea
Lazily looking straight at me
Wise old gecko on the wall
Waiting for flies to call
Hungry hyena having fun
Having a rest with a satisfied tum
Enormous rhinos running around
Entering late into their playground
Massive monkeys making noise
Making laughter with their toys
Elephant eating fruits and leaves
Even after eating bees
Dolphins are kept in big zoos
Deep into the ocean's blues
Bats use echoes from their squeaks
Beating others with their beaks
Animals, animals all around
In the sky and on the ground.

Thomas Russell (11)
Hulme Court Preparatory School

My Old Teacher

My old teacher
She walks the hall
Her big black shoes
She gives me the blues
And her long black hair
She was never very fair
And that's my old teacher.

Luke Kirkham (9)
Hulme Court Preparatory School

Chess

Move a knight
Put up a fight
Move your queen
Be really mean
Try and check
As well as wreck
Don't be too nice
Or you'll get a fright
Move your pieces about
Before the time runs out
Attack straight away
Or you'll be at bay
Fork him
Before he throws you in the bin
Attack now
Or you'll never say wow
Don't get in a mess
When you're playing chess.

Thomas Clements (10)
Hulme Court Preparatory School

My Teacher

Why my teacher's funny!
The way he rubs his tummy.
He has spiky hair,
That looks like fur.
He has big, black, bold shoes,
Which match his big, black gown.
He's so cool
And sits on a stool.
He always has a piece of chalk
And a whistle in his top pocket.

Sam Alexander Mellor (9)
Hulme Court Preparatory School

Spider, Spider, Hungry Spider

Spider, spider in his little web
Seeking food while he's still in bed
It's getting dark, why not call it a day?
But still hungrily he's seeking his prey

Waiting, waiting on his lace
Spun in secret in a dangerous place
Fooled by the breeze, still out of luck
All this waiting still no tuck

At last a quiver, a shake, a fly!
Finally some food, it's time to die
For the fly which struggles more and more
Entangles itself - death is sure.

The fly is wrapped in the beautiful lace,
To rot, to wait for the deadly embrace
From spider, no mercy will he give
For food and death is needed to live.

Sheik Raja (11)
Hulme Court Preparatory School

My Football Team

Pearson's strikers are the team to beat.
Playing up front is no mean feat.
Training hard in all kinds of weather.
The coach is tough, don't ruffle his feathers.
Is
It
Worth
It?
Am
I
Able?
Yes of course, we're top of the table.

James Craughwell (10)
Hulme Court Preparatory School

My Very Eager Mother Just Served Up Nine Pizzas

(This poem is the planets and the order in which they come, use it to remember them, you may have lots of fun)

My is for Mercury, the closest planet to the sun.
Not the hottest planet, that is next to come.

Very is for Venus, this really is the hottest.
Took a while to discover, but didn't take the longest.

Eager is for Earth, formed millions of years ago.
A place with many mountains, from which the rivers flow.

Mother is for Mars, the 'Red Planet' is its name.
Maybe we can live on it, though it wouldn't be the same.

Just is for Jupiter, the biggest planet of all.
Its gravity so powerful, its moons are at its call.

Served is for Saturn, known for all its rings.
The number of them seven, made of gas and other things.

Up is for Uranus, rolling round on its side
Because an object the size of Earth with it did collide.

Nine is for Neptune, with the fastest winds around.
2000 kilometres an hour in fact, must make a raging sound.

Pizzas is for Pluto, where it's always dark and cold
Because it is so very far away, it's difficult to behold.

Ameen Chekroud (9)
Hulme Court Preparatory School

Maths

Maths, maths everywhere
So much more to do
The easiest maths I have ever done
Has got to be 2 plus 2.

Daniel Murphy (10)
Hulme Court Preparatory School

Fast Cars

F ast cars,
O n Silverstone
R acing at 300 mph
M ichael Schumacher in his Ferrari
U sing his favourite car
L orenzo coming up on his left
A car with Montoya in on his right

O nly he can win this one
N o doubt about that
E veryone cheering as he races

R eally now the heat is on
A ll he cares about is winning
C an he race now better than ever
I n this Formula One battle
N obody else has a chance
G reat, he crosses the finish line in first.

Alex Claydon (11)
Hulme Court Preparatory School

A Bird

I am a bird
I have two wings
I have feathers on my body
I've learnt a lot of tunes that I sing
I dive and I fly
In the high above blue sky
With my wings going flap, flap, flap
I give Ben a swinging slap
My mouth is like the end of a tower
I go in the bird bath for a shower
My body is shaped like an aeroplane
I like flying over to Spain for the summer sun.

Luqman Mehboob (11)
Hulme Court Preparatory School

My Mate, Bilawal

My mate, Bilawal
Is so cool,
He acts clever, daft
And sometimes like a fool.

He is really funny
And in running he is top,
But when it comes to football,
He's a big flop.

He's an academic boy,
Always wanting to learn,
More, more and even more,
It's knowledge he does yearn.

Loads of people like him
And you should too,
If you don't, don't worry,
But he'll be looking for you!

Shamas Qumar (10)
Hulme Court Preparatory School

Death

Deep under the ground
Where the worms live
Here you won't be found

Deep, deep under the ground
Where the treasure is
You can hear your heart pound

Deep, deep, deep under the ground
You get hotter and hotter
Your voice is quiet, without a sound

Deep, deep, deep, deep under the ground
Where the coffin lies
The only sign above - an earthy mound.

Matthew Stocker (11)
Hulme Court Preparatory School

The Weird And Wonderful World

So bright, so beautiful in the summer
Not like winter and its absence of colour
Spring is symbolic of newness and life
But deathly autumn's the one I like

I imagine God, high above the sky
That's where I'd love to fly
Looking down controlling all I survey
Dictating the weather: what today?

The sky, always changing, I'll always love
I'll never forget that beautiful dove
So pure, so white, very mysterious
With a look on its face, ever so serious

The weird and wonderful world
Could give itself a twirl
I love it so much
I'd give it a touch
The weird and wonderful world.

Ryan Ellis (10)
Hulme Court Preparatory School

My Bedroom

My bedroom is a tip,
My clothes are on the floor.
The bin has not been touched
And my bags are blocking the door.

The bed hasn't been made,
My books are all around.
Mum says I should clean it,
Because you can hardly see the ground!

Handprints on the window
And shoes on my chair.
Sticky sweets on my desk,
Come in, if you dare!

Andrew Schofield (10)
Hulme Court Preparatory School

Snorkelling

Under the sea, as blue as can be
What will I see?
Is it a crab or is it a rock?
Let's go and look.

Under the sea, as blue as can be
What will I see?
Is it a flatfish or stone?
I will go alone.

Under the sea, as blue as can be
What will I see?
Is it a wreck or a trick of the light?
Will I be lucky? I might!

Under the sea, as blue as can be
What will I see?
Sand eels, scorpion, butterfish or blenny?
Surely it could be any!

Under the sea, as blue as can be
What will I see?
The water is clear, cool and very deep
So take a snorkel and have a peep.

Joshua Sayle (10)
Hulme Court Preparatory School

I Am A Wolf

I am a wolf
I live in the Gulf
Catch my prey
Then be on my way
Through the wood
Drinking blood
From animals I kill
With my will.

Chris Claydon (9)
Hulme Court Preparatory School

My New School

I started my new school today,
I can't say it's much fun,
We don't do work, we *never* play
And my teacher carries a gun!

I don't like my new classmates,
They push me around,
They're big and strong, lift heavy weights
And if I stare, they knock me to the ground!

Our windows are steel bars,
The classroom's always locked,
I can't even go to the loo,
Because the toilets are always blocked!

The food is pretty awful,
Soup and one bread roll,
But I'm told if I'm really good,
I'll get out on parole!

Our teacher says he's got some competitions,
They'll probably be for a prison cell,
He made me enter them,
So I know I won't do so well!

I guess I shouldn't have done it,
Shouldn't have committed that crime,
I'm not at school, this is prison isn't it?
I'm stuck in here for a long time!

Christopher Whitworth (10)
Hulme Court Preparatory School

Running

Running, running, I love running,
Over fields and on the track,
Thumping heart and aching back,
Adrenaline pumping, trainers stomping,
I love running . . .

William Lacey (10)
Hulme Court Preparatory School

Cricket Final

C ricket hero Andrew Flintoff plays a clever game
R unning between the wickets like a whippet
I n the interval Michael Vaughan says, 'Let's win this game!'
C unning little plan form Vaughan against his enemy Inzaman
K een to win, Kevin says, 'Well, we need to plot to win!'
E ngland looked well ahead, so they went easy on Pakistan
T hen you see Afridi trying to hit every ball for six

W hen the fans saw this, they were up and crazy
O n the game goes but nobody had a clue who was going to win
R azzak made 100 out of 40 balls, including 7 sixes and 12 fours
L ong time since a wicket
D uckworth-Lewis method came into the game and said, 'Pakistan
   have won the championship, yeah!'

Naqash Matloob (10)
Hulme Court Preparatory School

School

Back to school into Year 5
Will I come out of this year alive?
Reading, writing, science and maths
Football, cricket then off to the baths
History, geography, RE and art
Must learn my poem off by heart!

Into the playground, a break at last
The morning's lessons are in the past
What should we play, football or chase?
I'm on first, so take your place
The whistle blows, all too soon
Back to science and studying the moon

That's school!

Jonathan Lobley (9)
Hulme Court Preparatory School

Something In My Dreams

There is something special in my dreams,
I do not know what is in my dreams,
My favourite dream is that I could fly
Over the world.

I wish I had a fairy godmother,
Then I'd have a posh car,
I'd like a big house,
I would have my own bedroom.

I would live on my own,
I would live happily on my own,
I would still go and see my family,
I would go and see them every Sunday.

Charley Bezzina (7)
Limehurst CP School

Nightmare

There's something in my nightmare,
I don't know what it is,
I wonder what it might be.

It might be a dragon,
It might be a bear,
It might be a rat.

It's coming closer,
It's coming fast . . .
But it's only my sister!

Luke Davies (8)
Limehurst CP School

There's Something In My Bed

There's something in my bed,
Something soft in my bed,
Something with a round head,
Something red.
It might be a . . .
Bat,
Cat,
Rat.

There's something in my bed,
Something enormous in my bed,
Something with a square head,
Something blue.
It might be a . . .
Rabbit,
Mouse
Or even a bear.

I think I'll give up,
I think I'll have a look,
I might be scared . . .
It's only a book!

Emily Atherton (8)
Limehurst CP School

Bonfire Night

Get ready for Bonfire Night,
It's going to be a bright light,
It's going to be a big one,
My mum says, 'I'm having none of that!'
Smells of bonfire,
Backyard burning,
The leaves have stopped turning.

Aiden Kelly (8)
Limehurst CP School

Pets

All kinds of pets bring so much joy
For every mum, dad, girl and boy.
Dogs and cats and birds and fish,
Any kind of size you wish.

Some dogs are big, some dogs are small,
Some are like a fluffy ball.
Some are smart, some not so clever,
But they get you out whatever the weather.

Cats are cool and so laid back,
They come and go through their little flap.
Sometimes they come back with little gifts,
Like mice and birds and other bits.

Birds are small with bright colours and feathers,
They make such a noise when they all squawk together.
They never walk, they fly instead,
Wings help them fly around your head.

Lots of fish, not just gold, some big and bold,
Tropical, saltwater, hot and cold.
Koi, angels, placostimus, even upside down,
It's hard to count them when they are swimming round.

When I come home from school each day,
My pets are waiting there to play.
That's what makes the world so much fun,
There are perfect pets for everyone.

Charlotte Laskey (10)
Marsden CP School

Our World

The sky is blue,
The sun is yellow,
The clouds are white,
The moon is gold,
So try to take a view from the ground up to the sky.

Farah Araf (10)
Marsden CP School

Family Fun

A large family that's what we are
We normally can't even fit in one car

Happy and jolly most of the time
We all like the odd joke and a little rhyme

Parties at home are always fun
Always jumping, shouting, on the run

Loud music, games, lots to do
Old stuff and some that is new

Some people call it a house, we call it a zoo
We travel from Asda down to B&Q

Running from room to room, with joy and laughter
Our family really deserves a BAFTA

Lots of books are read
Sometimes in the morning, but better in bed

We're not allowed in the house to kick a ball
Because usually someone tends to fall

Lying around the floor are smelly socks
The doors at night have secure locks

I like music with number one hits
On my bed a teddy bear sits

Now I must finish my little rhyme
As I have completely run out of time.

Kasim Hussain (10)
Marsden CP School

A Haiku About The Sun

The sun is shining
It is a beautiful day
The sun makes me smile.

Sidra Alyas (10)
Marsden CP School

Hungry Fly

Fly: Buzz, buzz, what do I see?
something good to eat for me!

Boy: Horrible fly you can't eat my tea
it's only alright if you eat one pea.

Fly: Off I go but you can't stop me
I'll be back, just wait and see.

Boy: Don't come back
and get the food from my sack.

Fly: Off he goes, he can't see me
here is the food, so I'll have my tea.

Fly: Thank you for tea
now I'll fly away, you can't catch me.

Boy: Come back you naughty fly
I want to catch you, so don't go high.

Saresh Ilyas (10)
Marsden CP School

People Anywhere

Side to side, high and low
Round about in the snow

Babies with their dummies
Crying for their mummies

People on the street
Listening to the musical beat

People moving everywhere fast
Christmas is here at last.

Saana Ilyas (11)
Marsden CP School

I Wish I Was A Pirate

I wish I was a pirate
With a long thin beard
And a long big hat
With a sharp sliver cutlass
And my green parrot will be very clever

My boat will be strong as an elephant
A patch upon my eye
With a sharp golden sword
With a boat full of gold
A belt like a whip

My clothes smart and blue
With a pistol that goes *bang, bang, bang*
And a sword that goes *cut, cut, cut*
The sea as blue as my pants
And the sky blue of clouds.

Asim Ahmed (10)
Marsden CP School

The Darkness

It was night,
There was no light,
The bed was shaking
And my head was aching.
The door was banging,
Under the bed was clanging,
There was howling in the moonlight,
I was a frightened little kid
And the stairs were shaking
And the door opened with a bang,
Oh, it's only Mum and Dad.

Isaaq Mohammed (10)
Marsden CP School

My World

My name is Usman Ali,
I have a pleasant family,
My big brother's name is Hassan
And I have a little brother called Zeeshan.

My sister's name is Nadia,
She has a friend called Sadia,
My mum's name is Kishvar
And my dad's name is Saeed.

We live on a busy road,
A place where you can't get bored,
We live in a terrace house,
Which is too big for a mouse.

I go to Marsden School,
Where there is no place for a fool,
I go to the main mosque in Nelson
And I find out a lot in one lesson.

I love to play the PlayStation 2,
So I rarely go to the loo.
I sometimes play outside with my friends,
We play football around the bends.

I really like being a child,
For reasons that will make you go wild.
I must have all the fun now,
Before I decide when I will take a bow.

Usman Khan (10)
Marsden CP School

Chills In The Dead Of The Night!

A howling storm came shooting down,
Something about it was not right,
Following lightning came thunder sounds,
Chills in the dead of the night!

Terrible thoughts came to mind,
Rain thrashed down with all its might,
But there was more for us to find,
Chills in the dead of the night!

Something appeared on the glass of my window,
A scary figure with a blinding sight,
Followed by a tapping noise from my closet door,
Chills in the dead of the night!

Sophia Rehman (10)
Marsden CP School

A Frightening Night

There was no light,
I got a fright,
I saw a sight,
I curled up tight,
It looked like a bat
Or a man in a cape,
It must have been in my head,
So I went back to bed,
Then in the morning my mum said,
'Oh heck,
What are those two little holes in your neck?'

Shahjahan Aslam (10)
Marsden CP School

My Teachers

First teacher was Mrs Foster
She was really tall and kind
But what if she was mean
It never crossed my mind

Second came Mrs Dreamer
She was really nice
Talked mostly about maths
But always gave us letters on . . . *head lice!*

Next came Mrs Lonsdale
She was really thoughtful
But when it came to naughty children
She wasn't very hateful

Mrs Macines came next
Obsessed with model making
But when it came to art
She never did show us her drawings

Then came Years 4, 5 and 6
Mrs G and Mrs Pollard
They were quite the couple
But in the end they weren't really that hard.

Hassan Mahmood (10)
Marsden CP School

Rain

It started to rain
I was in such pain
I saw my friend
On a bend

I went to bed
Because my mum said
I saw the rain
And I went insane.

Ryan Richmond (10)
Marsden CP School

Teachers

Teachers are mad,
They are sad,
Sometime happy
Or maybe chatty.

Teachers are fat,
Might wear a hat,
Sometimes skinny
Or maybe chinny.

Teachers have a tin,
Won't survive without a bin,
They might have good handwriting,
Not so good at fighting.

Teachers may be educated,
But often hated,
They might like reading
And always like feeding.

For a child to succeed,
A teacher they will need,
They may get mad,
But good results make them glad.

Adnan Hussain (10)
Marsden CP School

Raining

It's raining
It's pouring
The maths class
Is boring
We stayed in bed
'Til half-past ten
All the class
Is snoring.

Kathryn Evans (10)
Marsden CP School

Sports

Cricket is my best sport,
Even though you need transport,
Pakistan is my best team,
Although it may not seem.

Football is excellent
And it contains the latest talent,
It is my second best sport,
But I never got taught
How to play the game, it was a shame,
Instead I taught myself the wonderful game.

Boxing is really great
It also has a great rate
My favourite boxer is Mohammed Ali
He flies like a butterfly
And stings like a bee.

Ibrahim Mahmood (10)
Marsden CP School

I Want To Have A Sports Car

I want to have a sports car,
A very expensive sports car,
It will cost a lot of money,
But I will drive it when it's sunny.

I would like to have a race
And bang out some bass,
I would drive at a great speed,
Then I'd have a great big lead.

I would like to have a car,
That was shaped like a star,
I just want to have a car.

Sufyan Iqbal (10)
Marsden CP School

Quick

I am a quick reader,
I like reading books,
I am the quickest reader in the school.
I read everything quickly,
I am the quickest writer ever,
I am the quickest talker ever,
I am the cleverest person ever.
Not really, I am the silliest person ever.

Mehvish Khan (10)
Marsden CP School

My Life

I love the sky
It's really high

The ground is down
But I love town

I hate brown
But I wish I wore the crown

I love games
Everyone gives me pain.

Sabah Kiani (10)
Marsden CP School

What Is Green?

What is green?
Green is the colour of grass outside.
Green is the colour of the fire exit signs.

What is green?
Green is the colour of the fireworks high.
Green is the colour of the birds flying by.

Michael Owen (10)
Our Lady's RC Primary School

Monday's Child

Monday's child is going to Hell,
Tuesday's child has a magic spell.
Wednesday's child is being a bully,
Thursday's child really hurt his bully.
Friday's child had an egg,
Saturday's child broke his leg.
The seventh child was all of those things,
But had shiny white wings.

Jordan Wood (10)
Our Lady's RC Primary School

Monday's Child

Monday's child is having a fight
Tuesday's child drinks Sunny Delight
Wednesday's child is forever biting
Thursday's child is like lightning
Friday's child had a dog
Saturday's child killed a frog
The seventh child jumped over a log
And landed head first in a bog.

Thomas Gray (10)
Our Lady's RC Primary School

A Week Of Teachers

Monday's teacher is called Mrs Smith,
Tuesday's teacher has got a sniff,
Wednesday's teacher is called Mrs Gray,
Thursday's teacher forgets to pray,
Friday's teacher is called Mr Barry,
Saturday's teacher has to marry
And the teacher that teaches on the seventh day
Is spotty and grumpy in every way.

Laura Holmes (10)
Our Lady's RC Primary School

Ten Things You Could Do With An Old Jar

Stick in a candle and use as a torch,
Use as a light in your front porch.
Use as a maraca and put in some rice
Or put on some numbers and use as a dice.
There are so many things you can do with this,
Such as turning it into a face and giving it a kiss.
Use it as a tub for putting in gel
Or use as a vomit pot especially for Mel.
Use as a winning stand just for a mouse
Or use as a little doll's house
And if you can't think of anything just leave it alone
And then I will use it as a dribbling cone.

Christian Jacobs (9)
Our Lady's RC Primary School

My Sister

My sister, Mary, is very hairy,
Some people think she's scary.
She is able to play the drums,
While she is adding up sums.
Her best friend is called James,
She plays board games when it rains.
My sister likes eating pasta,
She does athletics to make her faster.
My sister is nearly a teenager,
Oh no!

Patrick Smith (9)
Our Lady's RC Primary School

What Is Black?

Black is the mood
Of my sister at school.

The colour of my hair,
As wet as the pool.

I see the tyres
Of a brand new car.

The colour of a slug
On his way back home.

I go to the shop
And see black suits.

It's the colour of the skin
Of my friend from swimming.

Helen Richards (10)
Our Lady's RC Primary School

What Is Red?

Red are the lips when they glow,
Red is the roses that may grow.
Red is the colour of a skirt,
Red is the strawberries for Uncle Bert.
Red is the colour of a cat,
Red is the colour of a bright beer bar.
Red is the colour of a bunch of cherries,
What's your favourite colour?
Because mine is red.

Charlotte Taylor (10)
Our Lady's RC Primary School

Ten Things To Do With A Piece Of Girl's Hair

Make tooth floss,
Throw it away, that won't be a loss.
Make a flying hat,
Weave into a hat.
Sellotape to a bald man's head,
Stick to a woman's armpit,
Attract a nit.
Push it up your dad's nose,
Hold it in your hand and wait till the wind blows.
Feed it to a dog,
Or even the frog.

Caitlin O'Ryan (9)
Our Lady's RC Primary School

What Is Red?

Red is the fiery sun shining in the sky
Red is the colour of your heart beating inside
Red is a rose beautiful and bright
And red is a sunset going down at night
Red is the colour of blood dripping down
And red is not allowed to make a sound
Red is the colour of love and death
And red is the ink coming out of your pen
Red is quite a lot of things
And it will always be my favourite colour.

Jess Willcock (10)
Our Lady's RC Primary School

Minotaur

The flesh-ripping bull
He lived in a maze that was very gloomy
He got fourteen young women and men
And one of them was Prince Theseus

With one eye on sword
And one eye on string
He made his way through the labyrinth
And then he found the Minotaur

The Devil of demons
Who was as strong as a bulldozer
The mystic monster
With horns as sharp as a curved sword.

Molly Beswick (10)
Richard Durning's Endowed Primary School

Minotaur

This coal-black creature,
Sneaks down in the trembling maze,
He's caught one eye on pride
And one eye on defeat.

His muscles were boulders,
His roar was a booming hurricane,
His horns were daggers, weapons,
His charge was deadly as venom.

When he was angry, the ground would shake,
You could feel the terror through your feet,
He could not be beaten,
He was the king of the demons of the dark.

Emily Turner (10)
Richard Durning's Endowed Primary School

A Letter From Your Dear Nephew

Dear Auntie,
This week's been awful,
The weather's been ever so dull,
Bark Kent's been ill,
There's been a fire drill
And a terrible tomato soup spill,
(It left a horrendous stain),
Oh and my tights ripped again!
My flying power's failed,
Unfortunately on a skyscraper at the time,
Had to bail,
The Titanic needed extra power,
But at the time I was stuck up that tower,
Can't wait to jump into those furry PJs
And go to bed,
From your loving nephew - Superman.

George Warburton (10)
Richard Durning's Endowed Primary School

Minotaur

From the Greek goddess, the Minotaur sprang
His hoof upon Hell
Like Devil rang
His roar was louder than the most fierce storm
And through the labyrinth he would roam

The bull of the Devil
The monster of death
The mystical creature who gallops in Hades

His teeth were as sharp as a lion's claw
To help him rip up a human's jaw
He could not be exterminated by the sharpest spear
But he could make everyone fear!

Emily Cassell (10)
Richard Durning's Endowed Primary School

Superman's Letter

Dear Aunt,
This week was terrible!
On Monday I found a hole in my tights,
You could see my underpants,
It was just before I was about to save a pretty young girl.

On Tuesday I got stuck on the top floor of a skyscraper
And discovered I am scared of heights,
(It was the third time this month).

On Wednesday I got dumped by Tom Girl
Because she had been asked out by Batman.

On Thursday my flying powers went haywire
And I found myself flying round and round
In the most peculiar manner.

On Friday I tried to save the mayor
From a falling tree, but it landed on me
And I cut my knee.
The Mickey Mouse plaster has made ugly marks
On my lycra tights,
From your dear nephew
Superman.

Rachael Garner (10)
Richard Durning's Endowed Primary School

The Last Four Days In The Diary
Of Schoolboy Superman

Monday
Today I fought a T-rex
I lost of course
And broke both my legs
(I'm still in plaster)

Tuesday
I tried to save the town
Before I could
My pants fell down
(How embarrassing)

Wednesday
I tried to save Boscastle from a terrible flood
I couldn't help it
But I fell in the mud!
(I'll never get my cape clean!)

Thursday
Today I feel really bad
I'm giving up
So I put out an ad:
Superman costume for sale.

Tom Cowin (10)
Richard Durning's Endowed Primary School

Minotaur

Half human, half bull
The Minotaur fled under
King Minos' palace,
In a maze that
Nobody knows.

His teeth were like icicles, as sharp as razors,
His eyes were like glowing red devils,
His nostrils were like homes for a colony of ants,
His skull was like a ball of cement.

He could not be found,
He could not be seen,
He could not be beaten,
(Of that he thought),
One eye on victims,
One eye on death,
Theseus arrived
And was blessed.

Louise Bowyer (9)
Richard Durning's Endowed Primary School

Minotaur

Theseus' armour rattled with every step he took,
He knew that this monster would not bring him luck,
With his sword in one hand and his shield in the other,
Cretan bull, his father, Pasiphae his mother.

At last Theseus reached the centre,
With one eye on victory and one eye on defeat,
This evil monster only wanted his meat.
His horns were spears slashing the air,
His chest was muscley, huge and bare,
The warrior slashed him, stabbed him,
Until the devil of sorrow, pain and Hell was at last dead.

Emily Kingsford (10)
Richard Durning's Endowed Primary School

Spider-Man

Dear Mum,
I have had the worst week ever, this is what I did:

Monday
I lost my sticky pads,
I put them in the fridge
But they disappeared,
Perhaps the cat's got them.

Tuesday
I lost my flying powers,
They disappeared into thin air
I put them on the side
Or maybe on the chair

Wednesday
Where's my strength gone?
I definitely had it this morning
Because I was jumping roof to roof,
But this afternoon I couldn't make my own brew.

Thursday
This was a better day,
I found my sticky pads,
(They were in the fridge all the time),
But they are all frozen!
Resumed flying, hooray
And I lifted up a jumbo jet,
So it must have been my imagination
That my strength had gone.

Samantha Welch (10)
Richard Durning's Endowed Primary School

A Letter From Spider-Man

Dear Mum,
I've had a terrible day today,
I still haven't been able to climb that 4 metre wall.
That Dr Octopus, I still can't beat him,
(Well, I never could really).
Could you *please* sew my spider costume
Because I've ripped it in a very inappropriate place -
I would like you to find some more spiderwebs
Because I've run out
And now I can't trap anyone!
To top it all . . .
My X-ray vision has disappeared,
I tried to see what a bank robber was doing,
Somebody came and pulled off my mask,
So now everyone knows who I am!
Spider-Man xx
(Alias, your loving son).

Isabel Kingsford (9)
Richard Durning's Endowed Primary School

A Letter From Superman

Dear Mum,
I have been having a bad day today,
I am trying to save my best bud, Bob,
He is stuck on a high building,
(Seem to have lost the spring in my step).
Please can you sew up my costume,
I have a rip under my arm.
Also can you put a spring in it somewhere, too,
So I can rescue Bob, (he is still up there!)
I think I might as well hang up
My Superman costume for good!
See you soon,
Superman.

Laura Miller (9)
Richard Durning's Endowed Primary School

Minotaur

The flesh-ripping bull,
His hard, prickly horns,
The monster of the maze,
Demon of the dead,
His muscles stronger than terror.

He roared and grunted,
The vast desert shook with fear,
He padded the labyrinth,
Hoping for victory.

Half bull, half man,
He roamed around,
Until the day came,
A strong man called Theseus came along,
He struggled to fight him,
But the creature was dead.
He still roams around in Hell,
Looking for victims.

Lydia Tomlinson (9)
Richard Durning's Endowed Primary School

Minotaur

The Minotaur is a mythical monster
He lives in a labyrinth underneath the palace of Knossos
Which was owned by King Minos
It was in the island of Crete
He eats human flesh for his tea

The monstrous Minotaur has enormous sharp teeth
He has a head as fat as a giant boulder
His eyes are like giant marbles

He could not be murdered, he could not be killed
He could not even be found
One eye on goodness
And one eye on evil.

Jessica Moir (9)
Richard Durning's Endowed Primary School

Diary Of Batman

Monday
Got my cape caught on a power glider
While I was trying to fly, it's irreparable!

Tuesday
Had a terrible day today, my strength let me down
When I was trying to save someone from under a lorry
Granada television was there too

Wednesday
Well, today was the most embarrassing day of the week
I wet my pants when I was trying to fight Billy the bully

Thursday
Today I thought I took my problems quite well
Considering what happened
Robber Roger had just stolen all of Jolly Joke Shop's jokes
When I arrived he had got a gang of people
To trip me over when I was chasing him along the streets
Well of course, I cried (well, wouldn't you?)

Friday
Well, when I finally took my plaster off
It had left a terrible mark on my silky black pants
And I don't think it will ever come off.

Laura Preece (9)
Richard Durning's Endowed Primary School

A Letter From Superman

Dear Mum
I have had the worst week ever
Max Smith (who thinks he's evil Batman)
Bullied little Jo
And snatched Ben's candy
(What a bully)

I tried to stop him
But my teacher told me off, big time
And believe it or not
My teacher rang Auntie Elsie and told her

When I tried to climb up a tree to get a ball
(To impress my girlfriend)
Max Smith came with a long stick and prodded the ball
It came tumbling down just like that

My girlfriend knows I love her
But she walked off with Max Smith
Turned around and stuck her tongue out
I went as red as my tights!

Must finish because I've got to catch up
With my girlfriend and thump that Max Smith.

Love Superman.

Harriet Bowyer (9)
Richard Durning's Endowed Primary School

Minotaur

The king of the labyrinth under the palace,
He had teeth as sharp as a knife,
When he heard feet, he ran to the door,
He was stronger than a rhino.

He had eyes like curved marbles,
His head was like a mountain,
In the labyrinth he ran around, like a charging bull.

He had one eye on victory
And the other on pride,
He was the demon of death,
Then Theseus came to kill.

Then the creature was dead,
Theseus killed the minotaur
And got his success.

Jack Garner (10)
Richard Durning's Endowed Primary School

A Letter From Spider-Man

Dear Mum
I have had the worst day ever
I've been trying to climb that ten metre wall
For a year now
And I still haven't done it
I tried to swing to each building
And catch the robber
But I fell off the rope
I only got a few bruises
But I am alright now
I have got to iron my suit
Now ta-ra
From your loving son
Spider-Man.

Natalie Eccles (9)
Richard Durning's Endowed Primary School

Snow

Mummy, Mummy, when will it snow?
On my sledge I want to go.
Build a snowman big and fat,
Carrot, coal, Dad's old hat.
Feel the snowball in my hand,
Run, run fast, where will it land?
On your head or on your back,
Soft and sloppy,
Where will it splat?

Eleanor Parker (7)
St John's Catholic Primary School, Burscough

The Lonely Pony

I know a pony
That's very lonely.
I call him Tony,
Tony, the lonely pony.
If you should see him, love and kisses you should send
Because Tony, the lonely pony, needs a friend.

Georgina Pritchard (8)
St John's Catholic Primary School, Burscough

Loneliness

Loneliness is when you're trapped away from joy,
It's a life of sadness in a painful world of its own.
Its heart pounds to find love.
Loneliness is when you're lost on your own . . .
Forever and ever.

Alexandra Till (8)
St John's Catholic Primary School, Burscough

12 O'Clock

At 12 o'clock when the clock strikes,
Burglars come out for some loot.
Alarms sounding, windows smashing,
Then the car horn goes *hoot hoot!*

From down the road at number 12,
At a distant sight they were seen.
They'd rung the police, sirens are louder
And in a minute they were on the TV screen.

Photos clicking, reporters reporting,
As the police push the thieves into cars,
But when they get to the station,
They all have to go behind bars.

Emma Forshaw (8)
St John's Catholic Primary School, Burscough

About Me

When I was younger
I was as muddy as a pup
And I was always playing in the muck
Now I am older I love to scream and shout
But when I was younger I loved to run about
There are lots of things that I like
Especially riding on my bike
All my friends like to play
When we sing and dance all day.

Hannah Wilson (8)
St John's Catholic Primary School, Burscough

Jolly Holidays

The sand is golden like the sun,
The sea is gentle like blue skies,
It's also the colour of my pretty eyes.
That's what makes our holidays,
Delightful, jolly and joyful.

The sea can be rough and tough,
Just like an earthquake on the sea,
The sand will be wet and salty
From the salty water.
You will be surprised what you see,
The horrible salty sand
Created by the sea.

Maria Mir (8)
St John's Catholic Primary School, Burscough

My Motorbike

As I go on my motorbike
I roar up my engine
I feel the power as I build up more speed
Changing the gears as I go along
Skidding around the tight corner
The wheels begin to stretch
As I go around the bend
Brrmm, brrmm
As I go on my motorbike
With the greatest of speed.

Muneeb Mir (7)
St John's Catholic Primary School, Burscough

Fear

The colour is red,
Like
Blood streaming
Through your
Veins

It feels like
You're surrounded
By people
Glaring
At you

It reminds
Me of
Confusion
Like
Flashing colours
Flickering in
Your face.

Catherine Stevens (10)
St Mark's CE Primary School, Wigan

Sadness

Sadness is a dark tunnel of danger.
A prison of scared,
A whirlwind of watchers.
Sadness is trapped,
Terrified,
Shaking,
Running for its life.
Sadness is an evil earthquake,
Swallowing anyone,
Anything,
In its way.

Tanya Ratcliffe (10)
St Mark's CE Primary School, Wigan

Confusion

Confusion is sullen images,
Flashing in your half-closed eyes.
Not good
But bad.
Everything that's happened.

Confusion sounds silent
Like going down a deep,
Dark alley.
Hearing feet,
Scattering from side to side.
No one to be seen.

Confusion tastes like
Metal.
Pin-pricking
On your tongue.

Confusion reminds me of bullying.
People ganging up,
On one person
Who's confused
About what's happening in his life.

Bethany Sharkey (10)
St Mark's CE Primary School, Wigan

Mood Poem

Evil engulfing flames
Creeping towards you
Purple, red and black
Bulging in front of your eyes
Sounds like people
Trapped in a wall of shadows
Cold, shaking, waiting . . .
It tastes like the salt of lonely tears
And smells of the sweat of fear.
It could be bullying!

Thomas Janetis (10)
St Mark's CE Primary School, Wigan

Depression

Depression, what colour is it?
Is it red? Maybe green, old, dark,
Gloomy green, mouldy, fragile, fear green,
It's like fear crying, fragile fear.

What does it feel like?
A lonely boy being bullied,
A world full of loneliness, tiredness,
People screaming for help.

It smells like hungry, thirsty fear,
Rubber moving and smelly flavour.

It tastes like a smoky, misty,
Coiling taste sweet and chewy.

It reminds me of people
Banging things like tins,
People ganging up.

Chelsea Dempsey (10)
St Mark's CE Primary School, Wigan

Evil

Evil fiery eyes glaring at you
The colour of red
Like the Devil's curse
It sounds like the scream
Of lost souls
Screaming, screaming for help
It smells like burning rubble
And tastes like beetle juice
It feels like pain, suffering
Like a whirlwind of terror, torture
And devastating death.

Lucy Jennion (10)
St Mark's CE Primary School, Wigan

Anger

The colour is
Black and red,
Like burning hot flames
And flickering spits of hot coal fires
Red fireballs
Like the sweets
Exploding on my tongue
Ough! The smell
Burnt tarmac
And the smell of evil
So hot, so hot
Scattering feet
Across scratched dirty floors
Squashed people
Solid and dull
Altogether
Glance, glance
In anger.

Annya Stafford (10)
St Mark's CE Primary School, Wigan

Violence Is Against You

The colour of violence is
Red and black

It smells like smoke,
Flames and rain

It tastes like the smell of flames
It tastes like toxic smoke

It feels like pans banging
Against your heart
As anger
Beats inside you

It sounds like two adults fighting
And moaning in your ears.

Amy Sutton (10)
St Mark's CE Primary School, Wigan

Depression

The colour of depression is . . .
Dark purple
Like plums weeping
Black as a night with
No one around

Happiness, gone, gone forever
Nowhere to be found
A whirlwind
Sucking you in
Falling to the floor
The taste of dust
Trapped inside your teeth

It sounds like an empty house
Floorboards creaking
Silent
Lonely
Gone.

Georgina O'Leary (11)
St Mark's CE Primary School, Wigan

Anger

The colours of anger
Are red and purple all mixed together
It feels like a bullet hitting you
And you feel the full pain
The blood drops, hitting the floor
Like drops of lead
It tastes like something you taste the most
Something that will make you sick when you eat it
It smells like burning rubber that will choke you.

Matthew Cottle (10)
St Mark's CE Primary School, Wigan

Anger

Colour
The colour of anger is red
Like a huge erupting volcano
Flowing all over a village

Smell
The smell of anger is like
Melting, burning tyres in a junkyard
Piled to the top

Sound
The sound of anger is like everybody
Screaming
Screeching
And not stopping for hours

Feel
The feel of anger is like lava
Burning all over you
And somebody squeezing you tight

Taste
The taste of anger is like melting metal
Soaking through your lips
Then onto your tongue

Reminds
It reminds me of embarrassment
When you get a question wrong
Then everybody glares at you.

Adam Corless (10)
St Mark's CE Primary School, Wigan

Danger

Danger
Is the colour of
Dark purple
Like a tall turning twister
Coming right at you

Danger feels like an electric shock
Zapping through your veins

Danger reminds me of
A dead end
And there's nobody with you

Danger smells of damp bricks
And burnt newspaper

Danger sounds like two cats
Hissing at each other

Danger tastes like mouldy cheese
And dead rats in the alley.

Lauren Shaw (10)
St Mark's CE Primary School, Wigan

Anger

The colour of anger is red
Like blood
Running down your face like lightning
Like a boiling volcano
Making you scream
Rock hard bony knuckles hitting you endlessly
It tastes like bony teeth
Scratching down your throat
You can't stand the pain
Holding yourself
Hoping someone will rescue you
As your eyes slowly close.

Matthew Smith (10)
St Mark's CE Primary School, Wigan

Depression

The colour of depression is . . .
Dark seething purple, electric blue and black,
Like the midnight sky.
The colours weep,
Like slime, slowly.

It sounds like . . .
The moaning of a child in pain,
With nobody around to help.
It sounds like an echo,
From a blacked-out well.

It smells like . . .
An empty house,
Deserted,
For hundreds of years.
Dusty and creaky,
Dark and scary.

It tastes like . . .
Metal keys,
Squashed
Inside your mouth,
Unlocking devastating memories
In your mind.

Depression,
A dark illusion
Of a solitary figure,
In a still world.

Natalie Walters (10)
St Mark's CE Primary School, Wigan

Anger

Anger is a flame colour
Like a filled furnace
Burning your skin
The sound of anger is
Rats scattering noisily
Down the back alley
Parents shouting
Babies screaming
Anger feels like
Your eyeballs sticking out
Your body shaking
The urge to hit someone
Anger smells like
Burning paper
And burning tarmac
Anger tastes like
Red-hot chillies
Burning in your mouth
Fireballs melting on your tongue.

Jodie Sanford (10)
St Mark's CE Primary School, Wigan

Confusion

The colour of confusion is dark and puzzling
Like sudden footsteps behind you
But nobody's there!
An endless pain that feels like
Braces on your teeth
Being slowly tightened every weekend
Trees swaying madly, seeds spraying badly
Mad temptation urges out
He turns around but no one's about.

Chloe Dodd (11)
St Mark's CE Primary School, Wigan

Anger

The colour of anger is dark purple
Like blood dripping from your face
Making a puddle of blood
Beneath your feet

Anger tastes like burning metal
Sinking through your lips
And dissolving into your tongue
Like burning fireballs

It smells like burning glass
And rubber in a junkyard
And dust sniffed up from the floor

It reminds me of getting everything wrong
And being embarrassed
And everyone staring at me.

Jordan Croston (10)
St Mark's CE Primary School, Wigan

Fear

The colour of fear is
Black and red
Like the midnight sky
Turning red
It sounds like
The trees howling
Swaying
From side to side
It tastes like
A mouthful of bones
It smells like
Rotting leaves
It reminds me of
The woods
In the middle
Of the night!

Liam Simpson
St Mark's CE Primary School, Wigan

Nightmare

I had a nightmare!
I woke up!
I landed in a place that was strange
And guess what?
There was no football!
The old ladies grew flowers in the cup
The players were sacked
And the pitches were farmyards
The managers had different hair
So they were sacked too!
I woke up!
I was safe in my bed
It was just a nightmare!

Lewis Wilson (8)
St Mary's RC Primary School, Fleetwood

Auntie May

Auntie May found a flea
And put it in her tea!
The flea jumped out,
She gave a shout!
Here comes Grandad
With his shirt hanging out!

Ben Dollin (9)
St Mary's RC Primary School, Fleetwood

Shapes

Hexagon and octagon
Look almost the same
There's just one big difference
Their sides are not the same!

Katie Kerr (8)
St Mary's RC Primary School, Fleetwood

I'm Telling On You

'I'm telling on you'
'Why?'
'Because you stole my brolly
And you ate my lolly'
'They were in the trolley
Sitting with my dolly
That's why'
'I'm telling on you!'

Lauren Elizabeth Lynch (8)
St Mary's RC Primary School, Fleetwood

I Love Buddy

I love Buddy,
He plays with my cat.
I like watching them play.
They prance about
And roll around
And are the best of friends.

Bradley Evans (8)
St Mary's RC Primary School, Fleetwood

The Three Crabs

Here comes a crab
Ripping its claws
Here comes another
Heading for the shore
Here comes a final crab
Heading for the wall.

William Ferguson (7)
St Mary's RC Primary School, Fleetwood

Hate

Hate is red like flames of Hell.
Hate tastes like it is the 5th November
And someone has lit a scorching, blazing bonfire in my mouth.
Hate smells like the coldest, darkest tunnel going to Hell.
Hate reminds me of being in anger.
Hate looks like someone taking the mick out of me and rubbing
it in my face.
Hate sounds like someone being nasty to you and never
saying sorry to you.
Hate feels like your body is pumping up with bad blood.

Dean Stewart (9)
St Matthew's Catholic Primary School, Skelmersdale

Hate

Hate is red like a great ball of scorching, blazing fire
Hate reminds me of a face of doom and red fire
It feels like you really want to kill them really badly
Your heart keeps beating
It tastes like sour grapes and some stale eggs
It smells like red-hot chilli peppers
It sounds like a screaming girl.

Kieran McMullen
St Matthew's Catholic Primary School, Skelmersdale

Anger

Anger is red like the sun
It smells like drinking people's blood
It reminds me of the Devil's cry
It looks like a big ball of lava
It sounds like a pig drinking
It feels like something heavy on your leg.

Mitchell Alty (10)
St Matthew's Catholic Primary School, Skelmersdale

Love

Love is pink like a cute butterfly
It feels like your stomach going round with butterflies
It reminds me of my ex-girlfriend
With smoochy, smoochy
It's lovely, it tastes like melted chocolate
It smells like girly perfume
And boys' deodorant
It sounds like kissing and hugging
It looks like a lot of kissing.

Liam Hendry (9)
St Matthew's Catholic Primary School, Skelmersdale

Hunger

Hunger is white like a pale face crying for food.
Hunger feels like something banging on the inside of your belly
That grows and grows.
It smells like food fading away into the distance.
It tastes like the air we breathe.
It looks like people in a different, poorer country than ours,
Pleading for food.
It sounds like something asking for food.

Tommy Roscoe (9)
St Matthew's Catholic Primary School, Skelmersdale

Love

Love sounds like two lovebirds singing in a tree.
Love feels like a big pink heart.
Love reminds me of two people sitting in a love boat.
Love smells like a big, red rose.
Love looks like a flower with a heart in it.

Joel Granite (9)
St Matthew's Catholic Primary School, Skelmersdale

Fun

Fun is a rainbow like the most colourful and brightest umbrella
Fun looks like the happiest swan in the sky
Fun reminds me of a snowy-white Christmas
With all my family and friends
Fun tastes like a dozen flavours of ice cream
With a load of toppings
Fun smells like a soft lavender
And the most beautiful roses
Fun sounds like a big playground of happiness and laughter.

Stephanie Hewitt (9)
St Matthew's Catholic Primary School, Skelmersdale

Hate

Hate is black like a dry piece of ash.
It smells like a burning cigarette.
It tastes like eating one bulging heart that is still beating.
It looks like a burning face of hatred.
It reminds me of one big fight
With bulging guts spurting blood and knocked-out teeth.
It sounds like some red devils laughing with hatred.
It feels like your face being burnt by a hob.

Kieran Drennan (9)
St Matthew's Catholic Primary School, Skelmersdale

Darkness

Darkness is pitch-black like a deep, dark, filthy, slimy sewer.
Darkness reminds me of my dad's pitch-black hair.
Darkness tastes like wood, giving you splinters in your mouth.
Darkness smells like stinky, smelly, filthy rats.
Darkness feels like a black hole has just swallowed me up.
Darkness sounds like people screaming for help.
Darkness looks like a swirling black hole.

Shannon Donnelly (10)
St Matthew's Catholic Primary School, Skelmersdale

Anger

Anger is black like a massive black hole
Sucking up your happiness.
Anger has no face just like a snake's poison
It chooses its victim then dissolves
And makes you angrier than a mad bull!
Anger feels like a friend or member of your family betraying you.
Anger smells like a death omen
When you smell it, it makes you a victim of its pain and anger.
Anger tastes like an out of date chilli pepper.
Anger reminds me of a black dragon breathing its hot fire at me.
Anger sounds like a hurricane with a thousand people
Inside of it mocking me.

Daniel Birrell (9)
St Matthew's Catholic Primary School, Skelmersdale

Love

Love is yellow like a sunflower.
It looks like a big yellow flower.
It tastes like a ball of yellow water.
It smells like beautiful red roses.
It reminds me of a big red heart.
It sounds like a big sweet rose.
It feels like a lovely rose.

Olivia Don (9)
St Matthew's Catholic Primary School, Skelmersdale

Sadness

Sadness is blue like the sky.
It tastes very sad.
It looks like a ball in the fire.
It reminds me of spicy curry.
It smells like strawberries.
It sounds like I have a brick.

Zoe Treanor (9)
St Matthew's Catholic Primary School, Skelmersdale

Anger

Anger is black
Like the darkest hole,
It tastes like a block of sand.
It smells like a block of cheese.
It reminds me of someone batting me.
It looks like a ball of fire.
It sounds like someone eating with their mouth open.
It feels like you want to hit someone.

Leanne Sweeney (10)
St Matthew's Catholic Primary School, Skelmersdale

A Bit Of Snow On A Summer Day

A snowman stands in the garden,
Then the snowman said, 'Pardon.'
The white snow is falling down,
I haven't seen anyone frown,
I saw everyone's happy faces,
It's so crowded, I can't find space.

I built a snowman with a hat,
People were saying, 'Pat, pat, pat!'
My snowman had a scarf,
Then I cut him in half.
All the houses were very white,
So hold your baby very tight,
The snow is like a sleeping polar bear,
It looked like it had no hair.

Jessica Brocklehurst (10)
St Patrick's RC Primary School, Morecambe

About A Beach

I stand by the caves,
Gazing at the waves,
I stare at the sky,
I watch the crab walking by.
I love the beach, it's so much fun,
Just sitting here in the sun,
I love the fish,
I make a wish.

I play in the sea,
Ouch! I got stung by a bee,
All the seagulls fly around my head,
I would rather be in bed.
I love playing in the sand,
That's my land,
Babies are crying because it's so hot,
I had some water in a pot.

The beach is so much fun,
It's time for my friend to come,
My friend brought her daughter,
She loves to play in the water.
The sun is shining very low,
Come on, it's time to go.

Penny Jones (10)
St Patrick's RC Primary School, Morecambe

Snow

The snow starts to fall down and down
Until it covers the whole entire ground
You see the children up the street
Playing on their sledges

The cars slip along the road
Leaving the wheel prints
The snow is starting to disappear
The ground is normal now.

Rachael Brookes (10)
St Patrick's RC Primary School, Morecambe

The Snow

Children playing in the snow
Wearing wellies where they go
Trees blowing in the breeze
Wear a coat and don't freeze

Icicles dripping
Sledges slipping
The snow is white
Hold your hat tight

Children sliding down the hill
Mum inside, very ill
Dad cooking the roast dinner
That won't make us any thinner.

Anna Heath (10)
St Patrick's RC Primary School, Morecambe

The Snow

Snowmen are walking in the snow
It's falling low
It feels like ice
But looks so nice
The snowflakes like crystal sky

I watch the birds fly
I wake up in the morning
But I was still snoring
I play with the snow
But I'll make a snowman low.

Kirsty McLoughlin (10)
St Patrick's RC Primary School, Morecambe

Snow Poem

When the snow falls
It grows and grows
It's like white sheets of paper
People play all day

Marking the sheets with
Crisscross footprints
Children make snowmen
Cars making tyre prints

Snow glows in the dark
And the dogs bark
It's very, very cold
And children get told.

Francesca Wilson (11)
St Patrick's RC Primary School, Morecambe

The Devil

The fire burns all around me
I am stuck, nowhere to go
Just stuck
I wish I could get out
Every corner is guarded
The Devil taunts me
Over and over again
He teases and tortures
And never pleases, just puts you down
He said if I join him he will give me fortune
But I don't believe him.

Jordan Peters (10)
St Patrick's RC Primary School, Morecambe

I Made Some Jam In Heysham

I made some jam
In Heysham

I saw a hamster
In Lancaster

I saw a Rover
In Dover

I had a pool
In Blackpool

I had a dance
In France

I like the pork
In New York

I had a rest
In Skegness.

Emily Pearce (8)
St Peter's CE Primary School, Heysham

I Had Some Pasta In Lancaster

I had some pasta
In Lancaster,
I had some jam
In Heysham,
In Skegness
I made some mess,
In Blackpool
I went in the swimming pool,
I had one chance
To go to France,
I did nothing wrong
In Hong Kong.

Erica Pitcher (8)
St Peter's CE Primary School, Heysham

I Ate Some Ham In Heysham

I ate some ham
In Heysham,
I ate some pasta
In Lancaster,
I fell over
In Dover,
I went to school
In Blackpool,
I made a mess
In Skegness,
I forgot my fleece
In Greece,
I lost my pants
In France,
I got sent to the dungeon
In London,
I had a day
In Bombay,
I wanted to go home
In Rome,
And now I am home.

Carly Beckwith (8)
St Peter's CE Primary School, Heysham

I Fell Over In Dover

I fell over in Dover,
I spilt pasta in Lancaster,
On Sam from Heysham,
I made a mess in Skegness,
I went to school in Blackpool,
I got sent to the dungeon in London,
I went to Heaven in Devon,
I grew scales in Wales
But I can't get home!

Darcy Giles (8)
St Peter's CE Primary School, Heysham

The Magic Box

(Based on 'Magic Box' by Kit Wright)

I will put in my box . . .
A very fast motorbike,
A green pony,
The crown of a very pretty princess,
A jelly racing car,
A speedboat with sails
And a walking Man Utd top.

Literacy Group 5
St Peter's CE Primary School, Heysham

The Magic Box

(Based on 'Magic Box' by Kit Wright)

I will put in my box . . .
A pink horse with black spots on,
A tree with pizza and sweets on it,
A water zoo with people instead of animals
And a mountain with mops on it.

Jessica Fenton (8)
St Peter's CE Primary School, Heysham

The Magic Box

(Based on 'Magic Box' by Kit Wright)

I will put in my box . . .
An animal Olympics,
A pencil writing on its own,
A vampire singing
And an elephant playing water polo.

Richard Bell (7)
St Peter's CE Primary School, Heysham

The Magic Box
(Based on 'Magic Box' by Kit Wright)

I will put in the box . . .
A bright pink grass garden,
A green elephant with no trunk,
A parrot with no feathers,
A person with an apple stuck on his head,
A pig flying on a pair of scissors
And a little girl eating a cardboard box.

Jennifer Knowles (7)
St Peter's CE Primary School, Heysham

The Magic Box
(Based on 'Magic Box' by Kit Wright)

I will put in my box . . .
A pretty flower garden,
A humpback whale playing darts,
A giant marshmallow
And a horrible muddy football pitch.

Kate Rogers (7)
St Peter's CE Primary School, Heysham

The Magic Box
(Based on 'Magic Box' by Kit Wright)

I will put in my box . . .
A monkey on a bike,
A man on his head playing football,
Popcorn playing ice hockey
And an orange playing golf.

Matthew Guest (7)
St Peter's CE Primary School, Heysham

I Was A Fool In Blackpool

I was a fool
In Blackpool,
I bought a Rover
In Dover,
People called me Jess
In Skegness,
I ate some lamb
In Heysham,
I was in plaster
In Lancaster,
I made a band
In Scotland,
I painted my nails
In Wales,
It had to rain
In Spain,
And that's the end
Of my journey.

Katy Bates (8)
St Peter's CE Primary School, Heysham

I Ate Some Ham In Heysham

I ate some jam in Heysham,
I smelt a plaster in Lancaster,
I had a Rover in Dover,
I told a rule in Blackpool,
I made a mess in Skegness,
I saw some mud in Hollywood,
I saw some rain in Spain,
I wore my fleece in Greece,
I saw a cow in Moscow,
I saw a band in Scotland,
I saw pie land in Ireland,
I went through the phone to get home!

Emma Hutchinson (8)
St Peter's CE Primary School, Heysham

Thank You

Thank you for the world,
Thank you for the Earth,
Thank you for everything,
Thank you for my birth,
Thank you for my family,
Thank you for my friends,
Thank you for everything in the whole wide world,
Thank you for the animals,
Thank you for the trees,
Thank you for the mud,
Thank you for the leaves,
Thank you for my mum,
Thank you for my dad,
Thank you for my gran,
Thank you for my grandad,
Thank you for days,
Thank you for the nights,
Thank you for the shining stars
That twinkle all through the night.

Michael Mottram (7)
St Philip's RC Primary School, Salford

The Haunted House

Once in a haunted house
There was a mean and scary witch
Who had a horrid mouse
That night Miss Bean and Mr Pean
Came to the haunted house
They rang the bell
With something to sell
They said it was a new spell
When they entered the house
They were scared by a mouse
And the witch turned them both into grouses.

Niamh Hickey (7)
St Philip's RC Primary School, Salford

Hallowe'en

I love Hallowe'en
A time to dream
Of scary monsters
That gleam

To trick or treat
Up and down the street
And collect lots of yummy sweets

A knock at the door
And you go to explore
Who it could be
And then you see
A scary face staring back at me

Witches, ghosts and ghouls
Oh how we love to play the fools
Hallowe'en comes once a year
So celebrate and give a cheer.

Lucy Whittaker (7)
St Philip's RC Primary School, Salford

Hallowe'en

It was a cold winter's dark night
And a hooting owl gave me a fright,
I screamed so loud but no one cared,
The Hallowe'en man had made me scared.

He stood at the door so big and tall
And me before him slight and small,
His mask was so scary all wrinkled and torn,
I wished the Hallowe'en man had never been born.

Don't be afraid my little queen,
It's not really the man of Hallowe'en,
Behind the mask it's me, your dad,
That makes me feel safe and happy and glad.

Kellen Welch (7)
St Philip's RC Primary School, Salford

Jumping Frog, Morag

A frog sat on a log eating a brown Morag,
It ran away to the postman,
The postman said hello to the frog, Morag.
It jumped and jumped until it was night,
It went for its tea at half-past eight.
The frog was green with spots
And the Morag was white with no spots.
The Morag had half purple hair and half yellow
And the frog had no hair.

Megan Mitchell (7)
St Philip's RC Primary School, Salford

The Cat With The Hat

A cat wore a hat and sat on a mat,
Caught sight of a rat, so went to tell Pat,
Pat had made food, so they all ate their tea,
Then off they all went, so that Pat could see
There was the rat, sat by the door,
Chewing at crumbs, which had fallen on the floor,
Then the cat with the hat and Pat's own cat too,
Chased the rat off, to explore pastures new.

Liam Peers (7)
St Philip's RC Primary School, Salford

God's World

World, world, what a beautiful world
And isn't it so big,
From the tops of the mountains,
To the bottom of the sea,
Just look around and see what you can see,
All of your great creations with me.

Sean Doran (7)
St Philip's RC Primary School, Salford

Mr Giggles

I went home with the giggles
And that's why my name is Mr Giggles.

Mr Giggles had a great fall.

Mr Giggles saw a dog
And a cat.

Mr Giggles couldn't get up
For he was too fat!

Mason Considine (7)
St Philip's RC Primary School, Salford

My Pet Dog

My pet dog,
Jumps like a frog.
She makes me laugh,
When I am in the bath.
I love her so,
I want you to know.
She will wear a pretty bow,
So you will now see her,
Just shout, 'Go!'

Charlotte White (7)
St Philip's RC Primary School, Salford

Dogs

Dogs, dogs, I like dogs
They jump about like leaping frogs
Dogs, dogs
I like dogs
They love you
And they chew
On your shoe.

Jessica Wilcock (8)
St Philip's RC Primary School, Salford

A Spooky Night

Spooky, spooky, spooky night,
Spooky, spooky, spooky fright,
The sun goes in and the clouds come out,
The rain starts to pour as the lightning starts to roar.
Shadows come out to play and dance,
They knock on our windows,
They tap at our doors.
This spooky night
Really gives me a real fright,
This spooky night will not go,
No one gets any sleep,
So everybody takes one last peep at the light
Before they go to sleep.

Isabelle Kemp (10)
St Philip's RC Primary School, Salford

The Ghost

One day in Ghostland
There was a ghost
And he went in a train.
Someone said, 'What is your name?'
And the ghost said his name was Tom.
The ghost saw a cat and a rat
And took them to his home.
The cat liked the rat
And shared his bed and food with the rat.
The ghost was happy, he danced and sang,
He smiled happily to himself.
To share his joy he bought a toy,
So his friends could play.

Alexander Mayers (7)
St Philip's RC Primary School, Salford

Thunder! Lightning!

Thunder! Lightning! Bashing windows,
Scaring children,
Babies crying,
Neighbours howling,
Dogs barking.

Thunder! Lightning! Thunder! Lightning!
Thunder's scary,
Lightning's frightening,
Horror of thunder,
Horror of lightning,
Altogether they're really frightening.

Nicola Cuddy (10)
St Philip's RC Primary School, Salford

The Storm

The sun goes down and the sky goes dark,
The clouds come out and the dogs start to bark.

People rushing, buildings crushing,
Animals pushing and creatures not hushing,
All in the middle of the night.

Salvatore Briffa (10)
St Philip's RC Primary School, Salford

Poems

I have learnt to read and I have learnt to write.
I have learnt the difference between black and white,
But though I try as hard as I might,
I still haven't learnt to sleep by myself at night.
I know I rhyme but I don't mind.

Emily Litchfield (7)
St Philip's RC Primary School, Salford

All About Me

My name is Lewis and I am seven,
I have a sister and she is eleven,
I live at home with Mum and Dad,
I'm really happy and very glad,
I like to stand on my bed,
Upside down on my head,
I like watching telly
And putting sweets in my belly.
I have a robot,
So what!
I play games with my dad,
It makes me happy, never sad.
Sometimes we play chess,
He wins more and I win less,
Mum lets me watch Cartoon Network,
Only when I've done my homework.
I have a PlayStation,
With lots of games and lots of action,
I like to play out with my friends,
I hate it when it ends,
On Saturday we go to Asda,
It takes ages, I wish it was faster,
My best food is bacon and lettuce,
It tastes really nice.
Charlotte is my sister,
We play games like Twister,
We went on holiday to Spain,
It was far, we went on a plane,
We haven't got any pets like a cat
And that is that.

Lewis Conlan (7)
St Philip's RC Primary School, Salford

Love And Help

Love is good,
It is nice.
Put your heart in place,
Make your heart depend on it.
Are you doing your best?
Are you sure you help all the time?
Remember to be friendly,
Love everybody but trust God.
It is good to play but better to love and help,
Help your parents and help people who need help,
To be happy you need to love each other and help.

Tito Okanlami (7)
St Philip's RC Primary School, Salford

Lavenders

Lavenders are red
Lavenders are blue
Lavenders are green
And I like to stand on my head
Yes that is true
And I love you.

Annie Rose Hanily (7)
St Philip's RC Primary School, Salford

Animals

The cat and the dog
Sat on the log
The bear sat on a chair
The squirrel sat on a pillow
And the mouse ran into the house.

Victoria Ejgierd (7)
St Philip's RC Primary School, Salford

I Wish

I wish I was a pop star,
I wish I had a limo for a car,
I wish I had a mansion,
I wish I performed in concerts,
Most of all I wish I could sing.

I wish I was a football player,
I wish I was a striker
I wish I played for Manchester City,
I wish I was the best,
But most of all I wish I could play football.

I wish I was an Olympic swimmer,
I wish I was a winner,
I wish I was in the Olympic Games,
I wish I won the gold,
But most of all I wish I could swim.

Molly Stockton (11)
St Philip's RC Primary School, Salford

Stop War

War! War! War is bad,
War! War! Makes me sad,
War! War! Gives me a fright,
War! War! Brings no light.

Stop! Stop! Stop the war,
Stop! Stop! Stop it now!
Stop! Stop! Stop and think,
Stop! Stop! You will sink.

Help! Help! Help me please,
Help! Help! We need peace,
Help! Help! Stop the war,
Help! Help! Get them safe.

Rachel Kinlin (10)
St Philip's RC Primary School, Salford

Why?

Terrorists are shooting,
Children are screaming,
Why are they killing?
Why do they take hostages?

Politicians are arguing,
People are scared,
Why are they arguing?
Why are they scared? It's war.

People want peace,
They want no war.
Why can't the war stop?
Why, why can't it stop?

Peace will come, we know it,
Or will it come to world destruction?
Why can't peace come now?
We need peace before more war!

Áine Hughes (9)
St Philip's RC Primary School, Salford

Handstands

I went to my bed,
I stood on my head.

A cat sat on a log,
So did the dog.

I saw a bat,
So did the cat.

I stood on my head,
I had a red head.

Luke Bolton (8)
St Philip's RC Primary School, Salford

Rattle And Roll

Rattle and roll
Rattle and roll
Move it all around
Move it all around
Shake it all about
Shake it all about
Can you hear that sound?
Can you hear that sound?

Can you hear me now?
Can you hear me now?
I can hear you now
I can hear you now
It's a funky sound
It's a funky sound
Rock and roll
Rock and roll.

Dominique O'Kane (10)
St Philip's RC Primary School, Salford

The Jungle's River

The river went through the valley
And got deeper on the way.

The river was so windy,
I screamed with fright
And all I saw was the wind from the sky.

I was the only young boy near the river,
Looking and turning for clues.

At last I found my treasure
And leapt and cried with joy.

Cheta Anyanwa (10)
St Philip's RC Primary School, Salford

Autumn

Autumn nights
Dull, no light!
Windy and black
Let's go back!

Leaves are brown
In the cold town
Frosty nights
Lots of light

Warm clothes on
Shorts have gone
Crunching leaves
In the breeze.

Fionnuala Feeney (7)
St Philip's RC Primary School, Salford

My Poem

The bells rang,
The birds sang,
Down the country lane.
The children played,
The branches swayed,
Down the country lane.

The ladies talked,
The men walked,
Down the country lane.
The horses chewed,
The cows mooed,
Down the country lane.

Summer Redford (7)
St Philip's RC Primary School, Salford

God's World

Leopards pounce
Bunnies bounce
Worms wiggle
Caterpillars wriggle
Crocodiles snap
Cats nap
Swans glide
Lizards hide
Dolphins jump
Camels hump
Fish splash
Bulls' tails lash
Kittens play
Butterflies are gay
Wolves cry
Foxes are sly
Ants work
Anglerfish lurk
Dogs growl
Hyenas howl
Snakes slither
Peacocks quiver
Animals and creatures are everywhere
Look behind you . . . they might be there!
This is the end of my animal features
About all of God's beautiful creatures.

Olivia Flanagan (9)
St Philip's RC Primary School, Salford

War

War is a fright,
War is a jumble, mumble,
War is a crime,
War is a punishment.

Go to war, go to war,
He locked you up,
So give him ten bullets in his head,
He is dead.

Kill them all, kill them all,
Trap them in a hole,
Let them starve, let them be thirsty,
At last they are in rest.

I killed them, I killed them,
They killed my mother,
They deserve to be dead.

Billie Norrey (10)
St Philip's RC Primary School, Salford

My Family

My family is the best,
Better than all the rest,
They are sometimes mean,
But funny like Mr Bean.

We are a family of four,
We are not very poor,
I've got a mum,
Who loves making buns.

I've got a dad,
Who is really mad,
I've got a sister,
Who is really nice.

Sean McDonald (10)
St Philip's RC Primary School, Salford

My Hallowe'en Poem

It's Hallowe'en
And to be seen,
Are witches, cats
And leathery bats.

A full moon shining,
Werewolf pining,
Children trick or treat,
But *who* will get to eat?

I'm terrified,
Eyes opened wide,
My hair stands up on end,
Phew, it's just my friend!

Pumpkins glowing,
The wind is blowing,
I feel the time is right,
Let's go enjoy this night.

Holly Hargreaves (7)
St Philip's RC Primary School, Salford

Deadly War

Oh this deadly war,
All I can hear,
Gunshots and people crying and moaning.

Oh this deadly war,
How did it happen in the first place?
I've only got one thought, fright.

Oh this deadly war,
When will it stop?
Please, can you bring the soldiers home?

Ricky Jennings (9)
St Philip's RC Primary School, Salford

Conkers

Conkers are round
And dark brown
Autumn is cold
When the leaves fall

Conkers fall down
With leaves off trees
Gold, red and brown
All on the ground

Frosty in the autumn
Breezy and cold
People go home
Not very warm

Sit by the fire
It makes you tired
After your day
Of skip and play.

Alina-Faith Cameron (7)
St Philip's RC Primary School, Salford

Cats

The black cat sits on the wall,
Never moving at all.
With black, soft fur
And sharp, white teeth.
A long, wiggly tail
And small, pointy ears.
The black cat sits on the wall,
Never moving at all.

Brendan Kehoe (7)
St Philip's RC Primary School, Salford

Autumn Days

Autumn breeze,
On my knees,
Conkers fall,
Beside the wall.

Very cold,
Leaves are gold,
Better get back,
Before it gets black.

Very dark trees,
No more bees,
Nature's calling,
Leaves are falling.

Krystyna Kowalyszyn (8)
St Philip's RC Primary School, Salford

Autumn

Autumn leaves
On the trees
Crispy brown
On the ground

Red and gold
Now it's cold
Round and brown
Shiny conkers
All around

Crunching leaves
Everywhere
Golden brown
Such a good sound.

William Barr (8)
St Philip's RC Primary School, Salford

The Earth And Beyond

Compared to the sun
The Earth is the size of a ball
And so is Pluto
For it is so small

Living in space is a different matter
Things give us light
Look at the moon, it seems to get fatter
The moon is one of the things that gives us light
The little white spot we see
Is the moon

The moon is a lot bigger than we can be
We do not realise that it comes so soon
It leaves us a path
That we do not follow.

Alexander Mundy (11)
St Philip's RC Primary School, Salford

Trapped

As I sit looking out of my bedroom window,
Fire all around my house!
I jump inside my emergency room,
Without it I would be doomed.

It was morning and the fire had stopped,
I tried to open the door,
Help! Help! We're trapped!
'Shut up!' my brothers snapped.

Fire! Fire! in the room,
Then God had decided our true fate.

Rhiannon McDonough (10)
St Philip's RC Primary School, Salford

The Land Of Nod

When you're in the Land of Nod
Unicorns fly into the mist of the night
And when you wake, all around it's bright
In the Land of Nod

When you're in the Land of Nod
The fairies come out to play
And when they've finished their singing and dancing
It will be another day
In the Land of Nod

When you're in the Land of Nod
Nothing is a real bore
Except when your sister is having a great big snore
In the Land of Nod

When you're in the Land of Nod
All of your wishes come true
And that's what's in the Land of Nod
I'm sure you'll like it too
In the Land of Nod!

Rachael Lees (9)
St Philip's RC Primary School, Salford

Pooh And Friends Come Out To Play

Pooh and friends come out to play,
The moon does shine as bright as day,
Leave your supper and your sleep
And join your friends who jump and leap,
Come with a whoop and call,
Come with goodwill or not at all,
Up the ladders and down the tree,
A honey loaf will do us three,
You find the milk, I'll find the flour
And we'll have pudding in half an hour.

Abigail Spedding (10)
St Philip's RC Primary School, Salford

Sports

There are all kinds of sports
Kickboxing and karate
Jogging and jumping
Rugby and running

There are all kinds of sportswear
Little strappy vest tops
And very tight shorts
Lots of people take part in a race
As a rabbit hops

Some people are trained for races
Like running
And jumping over those big barrels
There are all kinds of sports, can't you see?

Grace Hanily (8)
St Philip's RC Primary School, Salford

Messy

Let's get messy, it's number one
Getting messy is really fun
Splitter, splatter everywhere
Mess over here, mess over there
Painting, cooking, creative art
Getting messy is the best part
You can make a real mess
Cutting, snipping and all the rest
I love mess, it's really cool
If you like it, you're no fool!

Erin Considine (8)
St Philip's RC Primary School, Salford

Goblins' Bridge

Under the big black bridge,
A goblin lurks out of sight,
When he sees someone in his sight,
He will grab them without fright.

No one knows what happens,
No one has a clue,
But every night someone's caught,
Just like the flu.

From this day, no one says anything about the bridge,
But every night someone's caught,
Just like the flu.

Callum Di Tonodo (10)
St Philip's RC Primary School, Salford

Why War?

War, war, why war?
It drifts through the nation like a thunderstorm,
People dying, children crying.
Why did we bring the horror of war to the country?
To America, to Britain, with Bush and Blair,
War, war, why war?
Not peace, not harmony but war, war, war.
That is all you hear on the TV,
Now hostages, but there is no peace anymore in this world,
Now people are homeless,
Just keep praying, praying, praying,
Please, for them.

Fenton Ludden (10)
St Philip's RC Primary School, Salford

Autumn

Crunching leaves,
In the breeze,
Conkers too,
I say, 'Boo!'

Cosy fire,
Very warm,
Sit by cat,
With a hat!

Leaves falling,
Cold outside,
Sometimes raining,
Sometimes bright!

Callum Consterdine (8)
St Philip's RC Primary School, Salford

Hallowe'en

Ghosts are white
Witches are green
They like to haunt you
At Hallowe'en
Robots march
Wizards spell
Sea monsters arch
And garbage smells
It was dark
I heard a scream
What a night for Hallowe'en.

Molli Whelan (8)
St Philip's RC Primary School, Salford

Frosty

Look at me
I'm frosty
I've no leaves
Because of the breeze

I'm bald because
Of the cold
I'm not ice
Because I'm nice

Autumn leaves
Fly in the breeze
Falling down
On the ground.

Aaron Sant (7)
St Philip's RC Primary School, Salford

All About Autumn

Red, brown, gold
It's so cold
Leaves crunching
Frogs munching

My dog barks
In the dark
Watch them fall
On the wall

Time for school
My writing tool
Nuts on the ground
Spinning around.

Stephanie Brimelow (8)
St Philip's RC Primary School, Salford

Autumn

Autumn is cold
The leaves are red
Orange and yellow
The dark evening is misty

The piles of leaves
Sway in the breeze
They fly in the air
As they fall

The wind blows
Through my brown hair
The frost is nearly everywhere
I sit at home, near the fire

I watch the fireworks
In the garden
They light up the black sky
Sparrows fly to the shelter of their nest.

Séan Baines (8)
St Philip's RC Primary School, Salford

An Autumn Day

Misty morning,
Leaves are falling,
The trees are bare,
Autumn is here.

Get home from school,
The weather is cool,
The fire is burning,
Whilst the rain is falling.

It's time for bed,
For old sleepyhead,
I dive under the sheets
And fall fast asleep.

Hannah McCormick (8)
St Philip's RC Primary School, Salford

Autumn

In the breeze
There are leaves,
In sky
Way up high.

Bites my nose,
Have I froze?
It'll be snow,
Oh no!

The colours to me
Makes me see,
Autumn is here,
Look at that tree!

Megan McKeown (8)
St Philip's RC Primary School, Salford

In The Autumn

Look at those leaves,
Moving in the breeze,
Blowing around,
On the ground.

It's going dark,
In the park,
Better get back,
Before it's pitch-black.

The fire's warm,
In my dorm,
I think of the park,
Now it's all dark!

Bethany Roach (7)
St Philip's RC Primary School, Salford

Leaves Forever

Leaves on the trees,
Leaves in the breeze,
Leaves on the floor,
Leaves try to roar.

Red, yellow and brown,
Leaves flutter on down,
All crisp and dry,
They hurry on by.

Leaves over the ground,
No grass is found,
The trees are bare,
The little girls stare.

When leaves are wet,
They're slippy I bet,
Leaves are better dry,
They go blowing by.

Charlotte Kierans (7)
St Philip's RC Primary School, Salford

Autumn Days

Conker fights
Breaking lights
Cold and dark
In the park

Children falling
Kids bawling
Babies crying
Parents trying

Dark and cold
Boys being bold
Conkers flying
Plants dying.

Heather Shelton (8)
St Philip's RC Primary School, Salford

Autumn Nature

Conker trees
Lots of leaves
In the trees
No more bees

Autumn leaves
Whizzing breeze
Golden leaves
In the breeze

On the ground
Squirrels dash round
There they go
Doing their show.

Colm Hughes (8)
St Philip's RC Primary School, Salford

Autumn Poem

Leaves are dying
Trees are crying
Autumn is here
So give a cheer

The air is cold
The wind is bold
We're back at school
So follow the rules

Colourful leaves
Fall off the trees
The autumn reign
When dark nights came.

Lewis Rowley (8)
St Philip's RC Primary School, Salford

Autumn's Here

Autumn is here
Winter's near
Torn up leaves
On the ground, in the breeze

Everything is brown
In the park, in town
The sky is dull
The clouds are full

It's warm near fires
Almost ready for snow tyres
The next season is coming
Ready for Christmas and good cheer.

Ben Mundy (8)
St Philip's RC Primary School, Salford

Autumn Poem

Rain falls more
Watch it pour
Sunshine less
Cold, oh yes!

Leaves turn brown
Makes me frown
Flowers die
Makes me sigh

Evergreen trees
Colder breeze
Birds south fly
While plants die.

Christian Oldham (8)
St Philip's RC Primary School, Salford

Just Autumn

Red and brown
On the ground
See the leaves
Fall off trees

Feel the breeze
Makes you sneeze!
See the mist
Make a wish

Fire burning
Weather turning
Conker fights
Last all night!

Annie-May Armstrong (8)
St Philip's RC Primary School, Salford

Autumn

Autumn breeze
In the leaves
Yellow and brown
On the ground

In the breeze
On the trees
Crunching leaves
Where it breathes

Trees are bare
Take good care
Leaves are wet
You could slip there!

Jessica Mannion (8)
St Philip's RC Primary School, Salford

Autumn

Autumn leaves
In the trees
Blowing through
Ninety trees

Autumn trees
Brown and green
There's a blue leaf
It's not green

Autumn days
Lots of delays
The bus is late
There's my mate.

Megan McDonough (9)
St Philip's RC Primary School, Salford

Autumn Poem

Autumn days
Are cold always
Rolling round
On the ground

Leaves flying
Plants dying
Conker fights
Last all night

Arrive home
On your own
Snuggle up tight
Night-night.

Abbie McDougall (9)
St Philip's RC Primary School, Salford

Autumn

Crunching leaves,
In the breeze,
Misty nights,
No fresh light.

Coloured leaves,
In the breeze,
Foggy days,
Long sunrays.

Clothes all warm,
In a storm,
Red and brown,
All around.

Anna Wynne (7)
St Philip's RC Primary School, Salford

Leaves

Leaves fall
To the ground
Children pounce on
The leaves we've found

Crunchy leaves fall
But we play on
We love to crunch leaves
All day long

Leaves are green
Some are brown
Others gold
A carpet on the ground.

Charlie Malpus (7)
St Philip's RC Primary School, Salford

War And Terrorism

Why does everybody fight?
Why can't they just see the light?
We're all just the same,
Why do these people attack again?

Why did we go to war?
It's only killing people,
People's homes are getting blown up,
They are becoming homeless.

Think of the attacks in America,
Don't you think that's enough?
All the people mourning
For their relatives.

Think about the people fighting,
Don't you think they've had enough?
Why do you like killing?
We're all just the same.

Callum Blance (10)
St Philip's RC Primary School, Salford

The Sound Keeper

When I walk along the street,
All I can hear is people's feet.
People chatting up and down,
Making noise all around.

The sound keeper has let the noise free,
And made everyone so happy!
Now the sound keeper is out for long,
Everyone join in with our sound keeper song.

Clap with us,
For as long as you can,
He is the sound keeper,
A very friendly man.

Jessica Whittingham (10)
St Philip's RC Primary School, Salford

My Family

M um, she is the best one you could get,
Y ou are seriously the best mum ever.

F or if I did not have my brother, I would not be in this class
A nd the same goes to my parents.
M y dad, well, he likes to go on my PlayStation and he
plays war games.
I like to play with his dog,
L ambert and Butler is my nana's favourite cigarettes.
Y et my family are not rich. We still have a great life.

Joe Crookes (9)
St Philip's RC Primary School, Salford

Wild West

In the wild west there are guns shooting
In the wild west there are bodies falling
In the wild west there are bullets flying
In the wild west there are horses riding
In the wild west there are people dying
In the wild west there are bulls fighting
In the wild west there are people crying
In the wild west there are cowboys attacking.

Ryan Robinson (10)
St Philip's RC Primary School, Salford

Heart Goes Bang

High excitement
Bouncing high
Up to the ceiling
I can't believe
This feeling.

Emma Lennon (10)
St Philip's RC Primary School, Salford

Dreaming

You get fed,
Then you go straight to bed.
The fairy tales take you away,
You dream about today,
With the dragons you slay
And you become the hero of the land.

Maybe you sail with pirates
Across the Red Sea,
Swim with sharks in the sunset
Or be royalty for the day
Or simply the everyday stuff.

Then it comes to where it all ends,
You wake up and go to school to see all your friends,
What will I dream about tonight?
We will have to wait till moonlight.

Amelia Wilcock (10)
St Philip's RC Primary School, Salford

Spain

Spain, Spain
It's boiling hot
Spain, Spain
I like it a lot

Spain, Spain
Oh there are beautiful beaches
Spain, Spain
Look at the creatures

Spain, Spain
What wonderful views!
Spain, Spain
What lovely news!

Jodie Malvern (9)
St Philip's RC Primary School, Salford

War And Peace

Why is there war?
People just want more and more
Why can't people not fight
And just see the light?
Not the dark
And don't make your mark

Peace is good
It is better than a flood
If only the world was like that
And no one would be sleeping on a mat.

Sophie Aulton (9)
St Philip's RC Primary School, Salford

Rainforest Life

In the tropical rainforest
Plants and insects grow
The singing bluebirds sound
Both high and low

When the rain starts falling
It trickles on plants and trees
And when the rain stops falling
A wind turns to a breeze.

Jenny Hanrahan (9)
St Philip's RC Primary School, Salford

Friendship

Don't walk behind me, so that I am the leader,
And don't walk in front of me, so that you are my defence,
Just walk by my side and we can tackle this together,
Every step of the way.

Sean Fielding (10)
St Philip's RC Primary School, Salford

My Family Poem

My name is Emily Whittaker
I am nine years old
I like the summer when it's warm
Because I hate the cold

My sister is called Lucy
She always moans
She is quite tall
My dad says she's grown

My dad is called David
He is six feet tall
He likes to go to Bury
To watch them play football

My mum's favourite colour is pink
It's the same colour as a pig
She works at the local Tesco
It is very big.

Emily Whittaker (9)
St Philip's RC Primary School, Salford

I'm Late!

I looked at the time,
I got out of bed,
I bumped my head.
I forgot my tie and had an inside-out shirt
And I couldn't even find my skirt.
I ran downstairs,
I had my breakfast as fast as I could,
Then I rushed to school
And fell in a puddle of mud.
I finally got there half an hour late
And then I realised it was Saturday!

Lucy Matthews (10)
St Philip's RC Primary School, Salford

Families

Families are people who understand you,
They are always there
When something's bad and true,
They help you through.

Sisters, sisters, I have two,
They may be annoying,
But they're there when I feel blue.

Parents, parents, they think they know the best!
But they're always there, even when I'm a pest.

This is my poem,
My family's the guests,
At the end of the day
I feel blessed.

Oliver Carroll (10)
St Philip's RC Primary School, Salford

Nice Animals

Hundle bundle
Animals tumble
Tigers here
Elephants there
Butterflies and bees everywhere

Lions in the grass
Snakes in the trees
Giraffes up high
Tarantulas eating big fat pie

Hedgehogs with their spiky backs
Parrots with colours that all match
Dragonflies that spin in the air
Big growly bears with very fair hair.

Orianne Lopuszansky (10)
St Philip's RC Primary School, Salford

Chocolate

Chocolate is dark, white and brown,
I put it in my mouth, it always goes down.
Better than chips, pizzas and sweets,
It's the best thing that's brown and ready to eat.
There's Cadbury's and Nestlé that makes my favourite food,
When I eat it, it makes me feel in a happy mood.
Chocolate is made in cakes and ice cream,
When I get it around my mouth, I lick it clean.
I would love to work in a Cadbury factory,
A chocolate taster, yes me.
At lunchtime, puddings are the best,
Chocolate pudding, better than the rest.
Chocolate galore,
I want more, more!
Brown eyes, brown hair, see how much we are alike,
I want chocolate instead of a bike.
So much to talk about, so little lines,
I could do lines as big as vines.
Chocolate is yummy,
Chocolate is scrummy.
But that's not all I have to say,
I love chocolate in every way.
Every time I eat it, I put on pounds,
Soon my belly's going to be on the ground.
Eclairs, Crunchie, Dairy Milk, don't go on,
Chocolate is the only one.
The brown yummy stuff,
Will always beat the cheese puff.
That's the end of my chocolate rhyme,
It's time for chocolate, yes I think it's time.

Katie Mannion (10)
St Philip's RC Primary School, Salford

Bubble And Stew

Witches breaking the peaceful darkness
Cackles and screams galore
But this is the way it has been on Hallowe'en
And will be for evermore

Watch what you say
Or else you could be in trouble
Carried away on broomsticks
Down, down to the witches' bubble

Bubble and stew, that's what they say
Every Hallowe'en night
Bubble and stew, bubble and stew
To disappear on the morning's light

Was that a cackle or just a creak?
Is the curtain hiding an evil old witch?
Bubble and stew, bubble and stew
In devilment witches are rich!

Is that you, Mum or Dad
Or is it an evil old hag?
Bubble and stew, bubble and stew
How the hours and minutes lag!

Oh no, that was a cackle!
Scream, shout and yell!
Bubble and stew, bubble and stew
Hello Witch, are you quite well?

Mum!
You horrid old thing!
Bubble and stew yourself!
Now I'll hide under the bird's wing . . .

Of my bed!

Lucy Higgins (9)
St Philip's RC Primary School, Salford

Speechless

Head dizzy
Aching head
Tired arms
Need a drink
Body sweating
Balls through
Red hands
Feeling tired
Throat dry
Lips cracked
Bat whacking
Heart pumping
Pulse faster
Got to stop
Jumping high
Throw balls
Over the fence.

Kate Anderson (9)
St Philip's RC Primary School, Salford

Lungs Go Pop

Football flying
Bounce to me
Goal ahead
Whistle blows
Free kick
To me
I shoot
I score
What a goal
Thigh aching
Fast movements.

Matthew O'Gorman (9)
St Philip's RC Primary School, Salford

Lungs Go Pop

Feet ache
Legs are tired
Kicking the ball
Very thirsty
Head sweating
Very hot
Can't run on
Score a goal
Everyone cheers
Feeling happy
One more goal
Heart beats
Faster and faster
Pulse going fast
Feel like falling
Try to score
Goalie saves some more
People cheer
People chasing
Up and down
Then I fall down.

Luca Di Stefano (9)
St Philip's RC Primary School, Salford

War

War, war, oh scary war
War, war, I've seen you before
War, war, you're scaring me
War, war, you're making us flee

You have trapped us in a hole
So you can have our souls
We are in so much pain
Because our country has lost again.

Liam O'Grady (10)
St Philip's RC Primary School, Salford

Lungs Go Pop

Breath goes
Sweaty toes
Lungs go pop
Wish you never done it
Painful heart
Lost from the start
Where is my water?
I need to fall down
I could just drown
I need a rest
I'm doing my best
Give me a rest
I can't run anymore
Anymore
Anymore
I can't run anymore.

Lauren Evans (10)
St Philip's RC Primary School, Salford

Lungs Ache

Shoulders ache
Hard tackle
Pass ball
Sore fingers
Get tackled
Suffer with pain
Get up, start again
Pass the ball to mate
Fall to the ground
And start to faint
Score a try
Parents cheer
Fall on the ground
And shed a tear.

Aaron Deasy (9)
St Philip's RC Primary School, Salford

Rules

Rules guide us through life
And help us through the daily strife.
They are made to protect,
So we must follow and be correct.

Rules tell us to do what is right
And give us sight,
To fill the world with love
And keep each country as peaceful as a dove.

But rules are broken
And evil words are spoken,
People go against each other
And everybody starts to suffer.

So let's follow the rules
At work and in school,
For rules guide us through life
And help us through the daily strife.
They are made to protect,
So we must follow and be correct.

Sean Smith (10)
St Philip's RC Primary School, Salford

Christmas

C hristmas is a time for cheer,
H appy times, your family's here,
R inging bells and singing songs,
I t's nearly here, it won't be long,
S anta will be on his way,
T aking presents on his sleigh,
M erry Christmas to you all
A nd Happy New Year, have a ball,
S leep tight and in the morning there will be
    presents under your tree.

Luke Lacey (9)
St Philip's RC Primary School, Salford

A Day In Nursery Rhyme Land

If you were to visit Nursery Rhyme Land, I bet that you would see:
Humpty Dumpty on his wall with Little Miss Muffet,
On her tuffet at his feet
And maybe even the spider that scared them both away.
You might see Little Boy Blue chasing the sheep and cows,
Or the Duke of York and his marching men.

You may even see Mary in her garden or Jack and Jill,
On that hill, putting blackbirds in a pie,
For the pussy cat,
Who was chasing the Little Mouse Brown up the clock,
While Tommy Tucker sang for his supper (some of Jack Horner's pie).

Johnny is hungry too because he was on his see-saw all day
And Jack Sprat's sharing with Old King Cole,
As the children go out to play
And watch the cow jump over the moon,
Whisking a fly from her tail.

Maybe Old Mother Hubbard catching the nine-thirty train
Or the black sheep selling wool to the boy who lives down the lane
And for Mother Goose to make a scarf for the pig,
Home again, home again, jiggety-jig.

A crooked man or a baker's man run and run,
See if you can beat Jumping Joan,
Cobbler, cobbler mend my shoe, do it quicker than Jack or Sue,
Or quicker than the weasel!

Jack is jumping over the candlestick,
Somebody stop him, quick, quick, quick!

If you were to visit Nursery Rhyme Land,
There is so much for you to see,
But you wouldn't catch me there,
No siree!

Kate Jones (9)
St Philip's RC Primary School, Salford

The Battle

When the wind is a ghostly echo, upon a bed of stars,
When the moonlight silhouettes those who prepare to charge.
When the silence is unbearable the men can take no more,
That's when the dreaded enemy beat on the castle door.
A thousand hearts beat wildly, a thousand breaths are held,
As each and every comrade wonders which ones will be felled.
From the distant darkness, a lonely bugle sounds,
Showers of flaming arrows pierce the frosty ground.
The battle now commences, with screams and shouts and roars,
The axemen wield their axes; the swordsmen wield their swords.
Archers lose their arrows, they fall with deadly aim,
Charging knights on horseback rise up to do the same.
Ferocious was the battle in which many men were slain,
But victory was triumphant, so all was not in vain.

Matthew Woodhead (10)
St Philip's RC Primary School, Salford

Hallowe'en

Hallowe'en is such a scream
You can dress up as a ghost
Which is scarier than most
At night we go trick-or-treating
And the sweets we get, we end up eating

Don't answer the door because we will scare
We are little monsters and we don't care
When we come home, we eat burgers and apples we dunk
Then we take off our costumes and put them in a trunk
We kiss our mum goodnight
Then shout 'Boo!' for one last fright.

Melanie Cleary (7)
St Philip's RC Primary School, Salford

Months Of The Year

January brings your face aglow,
having fun in the snow.

February brings a shiver,
having a hot roast dinner.

March brings a colourful flower,
the sun shining with all its power.

April brings an Easter bunny,
it starts to get more sunny.

May brings a garden of flowers,
no sign of any showers.

June brings a cool drink,
washing yourself down in the sink.

July brings August near,
walking on the pier.

August brings the orange sun,
children playing, having fun.

September brings a pencil and pen,
working hard again and again.

October brings a cold breeze,
children playing picking leaves.

November brings Bonfire Night,
all is set alight.

December brings Christmas Day,
hip, hip, hooray!

Keeley Murray (9)
St Philip's RC Primary School, Salford

Spooky Spider

I am a spooky spider
and I live under Simon's bed,
I eat apples and bananas
that are kept on the window ledge.

When I wake up in the morning,
I crawl under the door
and make my way towards the cheese,
which is lying on the floor.

Some people say I'm hairy,
some people say I'm small,
but I'm the *spooky spider!*
I'm not like that at all.

My webs are huge,
they are massive,
they hang over the door,
but the other day
someone swept me away
and I fell onto the floor.

I don't eat flies,
they are nasty,
but by george!
meat pasties are good!

Now remember,
I'm a spooky spider
that lives under Simon's bed!

Jessica Gillibrand (10)
St Philip's RC Primary School, Salford

The Oak Tree In My Garden

My oak tree in my garden
is a sailing ship anchored in the deep sea.

My oak tree in my garden
is a Viking ship thick as can be.

My oak tree in my garden
has a smiley curve in its trunk
because the singing birds live in its long, strong branches.

My oak tree in my garden
is surrounded by red roses
like he is the king of flowers.

My oak tree in my garden
looks through my bedroom window
to make sure I'm safe and well.

My oak tree is beautiful.

Amelia Thomas-Wilson (9)
St Philip's RC Primary School, Salford

A Poem On A Midnight War

The stars are brighter than the sun,
The moon is as round as a bun,
Little animals walk on the pointy grass at night,
It is as quiet as a mouse on tiptoe.

Bang, bang go the guns of men,
Boom, boom go the cars exploding,
Screams come from men and women,
Crying from little babies.

Mothers running with babies in their hands,
Trying to find a safe place,
Men attacking the soldiers,
Children dying by gunshots.

Ben Whelan (9)
St Philip's RC Primary School, Salford

The Wicked Old Witch

There was a wicked old witch,
Who lived in a house in the wood,
She only came out at night
And frightened people whenever she could.

Her face was wrinkled and green
And was horrible to be seen.
Her nose was crooked and bent,
Covered in warts and blackheads.

She rode upon a broom,
Chanting, 'I'll get you soon,
I'll put you in my pot,
Full of frogs, toads and snot.'

She flew round the sky with her black cat
And wore a silly old hat,
When daylight came,
She went back to bed again.

Kayleigh Williams (11)
St Philip's RC Primary School, Salford

Silver Daisy, Buttercup Gold

Silvery daisy, buttercup gold
Here they gleam for us all to hold
Yellow and white, the meadows shine
With silver and gold that is yours and mine!

Treasure that cannot be hidden away
Gold which nobody's money can pay
Wealth that's yours and mine to share
And store in our memories, rich and rare

Dance in the meadows, we've gold on our shoe!
Pluck a few daisies, there's silver for you!
We've far more riches than we can hold!
With big moon daisies and buttercup gold!

Ariana Lytwyn (9)
St Philip's RC Primary School, Salford

Exercise

Dry lips
Sweat drips
Throat dry
Ready to die
Muscles ache
Got to win
One more point
Eyes going dim
Ball shoots back
Arm swings back
Got to wake
I've got the ball
People run down
The hall
I need to rest
Got to do
My best.

Claire Reilly (9)
St Philip's RC Primary School, Salford

Football Crazy

Heart beating
Really fast
Dry throat
Need to stop
Lips dry
Need to stop
Sweat strolling
Teeth crackling
Really hard
Muscle banging
Throat hurting
From shouting.

Fabio Hilton (9)
St Philip's RC Primary School, Salford

Gut Buster

Legs ache
Swallowing water
Heart beating
Faster and faster
Feet kicking
Out of the water
Sweat dribbling
Feeling happy
A little sad
Dashing arms
Legs ache
Swallowing water
Heart beating
Faster and faster.

Pierce Woods (9)
St Philip's RC Primary School, Salford

Lungs

Football in
The goal,
Lungs go pop,
Rain goes drip,
Spine goes crack,
Past people,
Passing up
And down,
Then I fall down
On the ground!
Get kicked
In the leg.

Aaron Ruddin (10)
St Philip's RC Primary School, Salford

Catching My Breath

Legs aching
Back bent
Blood pumping
Sweat dripping
Lungs breathless
Heart pounding
No more please
I'm nearly there
One more point
Legs aching
Back bent
Blood pumping
Sweat dripping
Lungs breathless
Heart pounding
Yes, I've done it!

Samantha Kemp (9)
St Philip's RC Primary School, Salford

Heart Pumping

Head aching,
Heart pumping,
Mouth bleeding
And very dry.
Eyes dripping,
Like when you cry,
Arms swinging,
One more knock-out,
To win the match.
Dodging the punch,
Punching back.

Jack McGill (9)
St Philip's RC Primary School, Salford

Need Water!

Arms killing
Feet flop
Mouth filling
Need water
Lungs full
Rolling over
Need to pull
Myself up
Back-flip
Slide down
Start to tip
Upside-down
Spin over
The bar
I almost
Flew very far
Trying to leap
For a star
Heading for
A new car.

Carys Laing (9)
St Philip's RC Primary School, Salford

Dire Though

Feet kicking
Legs tired
Need water
Head sweating
Heart and pulse
Beating like a drum
Think I'm going to faint
Got to score a goal
The crowd goes
Wild, hooray
We scored.

Declan Ferguson (9)
St Philip's RC Primary School, Salford

Breathless

Lungs hurt
Feet sore
Very tired
I'm admired
Need water
Aching of thirst
I'm going to burst
Sweaty hands
I saw bands
Play in sand
Legs hurt
Growing pains start
I like Bart
Kicking a ball
He is tall
Legs whacking
I like goaling
Also bowling
Feet kicking.

John Zamojskyj (9)
St Philip's RC Primary School, Salford

Lungs Go Pop

Muscles weak
Heart pumping
Out of breath
Sore eyes
Legs flapping
Arms killing
Lungs pumping
Throat soar
Dry lips
Getting hotter
Dizzy head.

Niamh Harrington (9)
St Philip's RC Primary School, Salford

Energy Needed

Breathe badly
Head aches
Lifting legs
Arms up
Sweaty nose
Drip drop
Wet clothes
Trying hard
Ready to pop
In the school yard
In the grass
Keeping up running
Fast heart
Needs energy.

Saskia Swarbrick (9)
St Philip's RC Primary School, Salford

Black Lungs

Quick fist
Flying through
Legs intense
Arm intense
Sweat dripping
Like pouring rain
On my head
Chest heavy
Strong hits
Taking in
Lungs exploding
Heart beating
Faster and faster.

Loga Di Tondon (9)
St Philip's RC Primary School, Salford

Heartbeat

Legs aching
Heart beating
Too fast
Head down
Need water
Throat dry
Run down the line
Sweat drips
Cross in
Header saved
Rain coming down
Hard

Strike at goal
Top corner
Goal scored
Five-nil
To us.

Kieran Tierney (9)
St Philip's RC Primary School, Salford

Tired

Arms aching
Legs hurt
Sweat dripping
Down face
Hands hurting
Legs kicking
Fist clash
Legs high
Karate chops
Muscles grow
Flying kicks
Dragon punch
Crescent kick.

Paul Coughlin (9)
St Philip's RC Primary School, Salford

The Storm

The thunderstorm roars, you can see its claws,
The thunder clapped against the rain,
You should have seen the people's pain.
People running to save themselves,
The thunder collided against a house,
People do not like the thunder,
So they hid right under,
The thunder whispers, 'Don't be afraid!'
But the people just didn't listen.
The thunder peeks, the thunder seeks,
Someone crying beneath the shelter,
'I really, really don't like the thunder.'
The thunder howled, the thunder cried,
It had really big black eyes.
'I don't know why you don't like me,
I am just like you,
Can I just tell you
That I have the same features,
I have the same life,
It's just that I am a different colour,
Why is that such a problem in life?'

Laura Elford-O'Dowd (10)
Sacred Heart Catholic Primary School

Flowers And Clouds

I'll sit here forever picking the flowers,
I've sat here watching the shapes go by,
I've seen a horse, a house, a fly,
I've seen a dragon pass by,
I've picked a daisy, blossom and bluebell,
Why are they nice, flowers and clouds?
The hours have soon passed by.

Charmaine Johnson (10)
Sacred Heart Catholic Primary School

The Matches

From Dundee to Dover,
The matches are over.
If anyone's lost,
They'll be counting the cost.

Over at Rovers they thought they had won,
Then came City and made them feel glum.
Norwich City, oh what a pity,
Oh dear me, we might have to employ a kitty.

Over at Highbury, the Magpies just flew,
Oh you can tell the Palace are new,
United now hardly can stand,
Over in the goalmouth, right into the sand.

Life's not worth a carrot,
When you're sick as a parrot.
That's all I can say,
About football today.

Joseph Jolly (10)
Sacred Heart Catholic Primary School

Fire

The fire is as hot as a face filled with rage,
It could burn through this very page.
It runs through the flammable objects,
After all, that is their favourite subjects.
It may just rush through the night
And give the people an awful fright.
All we need is a fire engine there,
To give the fire a little scare.
We hosed him out,
Before he could shout,
'Please don't put me out!'

Charles Iddon (10)
Sacred Heart Catholic Primary School

The Wizard, Jack Frost!

The wizard, Jack Frost is here again,
Icing up the windowpane,
Scribbles away the whole night long,
Dancing and singing his icy song.

In the morning as we wake,
We gaze upon his frosty cape.
As we breathe upon his art,
We slowly watch the melting start.

Into the sky comes Mr Sun
And poor Jack Frost will soon be glum.
Now the rain is on its way,
I guess just like any other day.

Victoria Tootell (10)
Sacred Heart Catholic Primary School

Teddy Bear

He sleeps by night
And plays by day,
And all of this is whilst I'm away.
Sometimes he comes and cuddles me,
But that is because he isn't a bumblebee.
He has a picnic with his friends,
Just as the week is about to end.
As I come home for my tea,
I'm glad that bear has made some
Just for *me!*

Lucy Parkinson (10)
Sacred Heart Catholic Primary School

Mr Alucard

Last night I woke up late,
With a shock to find outside,
Mr Alucard
Was staring and glaring inside.
In the morning I woke up,
I thought it was all a dream,
But when I walked outside the door,
You'll never guess what I saw,
I walked past the window to see,
Red water running towards me.
I stayed awake all night having an idea,
That Mr Alucard is actually
Dracula!

Nicola Blackledge (10)
Sacred Heart Catholic Primary School

Water

Shouting down the long, long streams it was
Water
Running down from the river, yes it is
Water
Screaming and crashing on all the waves, yes it is
Water
Quiet laying in the pond, yes it is
Water
Staring up the stars at night from the dull sea, yes it is
Water
Falling from the skies above all the rain
And that's water!

Bethany McMullan (10)
Sacred Heart Catholic Primary School

The Silver Moon

When the light is dark,
He watches us leaving the park,
When the moon takes over the sun,
He starts his job and has lots of fun.
When we are sleeping, the moon is wide awake
And then we wake up to a rushing lake,
When morning comes and we are fed,
The moon is tucked up in bed.

Leah Westwater (10)
Sacred Heart Catholic Primary School

Chocolate Cake

I love chocolate cake
It makes me go all mad
Its spongy middle takes me in
And makes me really glad
Its chocolaty coat makes
Me chocolate myself
All I know, it's not good
For my health.

Shannon Jones (10)
Sacred Heart Catholic Primary School

Wind

Wind pushes you,
Wind whistles at you,
Wind pokes you in the eyes,
When you stare at it,
Wind will push you if
You walk down that street.

Stephen Sumner (11)
Sacred Heart Catholic Primary School

The Bully

I know a boy in my class,
Who is a big bully,
When he plays tig,
Everyone is in a hurry!
He shouts and screams
And everyone takes cover,
He sometimes makes people cry
To their mothers.

Henry Linn (10)
Sacred Heart Catholic Primary School

Happiness

Happiness is yellow like the sun on a summer morning,
It tastes like sausage and chips,
Fresh from the chip shop.
It looks like joy,
It sounds like laughter,
It smells like chocolate,
Fresh from the packet.
Happiness feels like today.

Toby Gratrix (7)
Singleton CE Primary School

Love

Love is a sensitive colour red.
It sounds like sea waves running down my hair.
It smells like a strawberry so eager to eat.
It tastes like a blackberry dripping down your chin.
It feels like a hug from the bestest mum.
It looks like a field of beautiful golden corn
And it reminds me of the rainbow.

Bethany Tomlinson (10)
Singleton CE Primary School

Hate

The taste of hate is a poisonous sprout
Gnawing away at your insides.
The colour of hate is a black hole
Sucking up the world forever.
The smell of hate is a cold dead fish
Decaying on the beach for weeks.
Hate reminds me of robbers and thieves
Stealing and breaking everything.
The texture of hate is a sharp, bloody knife
Cutting and stabbing again and again.
The sound of hate is a piercing screech,
Sending a shiver down my spine.
Hate looks like an arrow speeding towards you.
Hate could take over your mind.
Make sure it doesn't.

Josh Powlesland (10)
Singleton CE Primary School

Hate

Hate is as red as the fires of Hell,
burning a hole through your body.
Hate looks like a hooded man
rattling bars in prison.
Hate feels like being stabbed
by a red, bloody knife.
Hate tastes like blood
squeezed out of a diseased cow.
Hate reminds me of a black hole
sucking all in its path into eternal darkness.
Hate smells like a bowl of rotten eggs
boiled in scalding hot water.

Greg Richardson (10)
Singleton CE Primary School

Love

Love is the colour of rosy, pale pink roses
standing in the yellow, glinting sun.

It tastes like hot chocolate running smoothly
down my throat on a cold night
while sitting by the fire in a very comfy chair.

It sounds like little bluebirds singing in the
dawn of morning in a well-tuned voice.

It smells like fresh lavender in a garden
full of flowers so beautiful to look at.

It reminds me of my daddy tucking me up
in my bed and the feel of going to sleep
and getting warm under my thick duvet.

It feels like the soft coat of a Labrador dog
sitting near the fire on a cold night.

It looks like a little egg,
hatching in the nest of a big, old oak tree.

Katie Davies (9)
Singleton CE Primary School

Happiness

Happiness is the colour of the sun setting
in the distance whilst watching television.

It sounds like a bird whistling really loudly.

It smells like pasta and warm sausages,
the smell of pancakes with sugar on them.

It tastes like a burger with salad and sauce.

It feels like someone is giving me a message.

It looks like a football team I cheer on, scoring a goal.

It reminds me of myself bouncing on my trampoline,
doing a somersault.

Harry Heywood (9)
Singleton CE Primary School

Silence

Stop for a while and let your mind wander,
diving into a pool of long-lost memories and dreams.

Silence is good, silence is bad,
silence is wondrous, silence is mad!

Silence is bottles of peace being poured
into a lavender pool of fresh water.

Silence tastes like plain boring chocolates
with strawberry and kiwi-flavoured fizzy popping water.

Silence looks like beautiful fish just swimming towards me,
in a glass see-through fish tank with glittering sparkles
just waiting to be seen.

Silence looks like a broken television
fizzing and blurring.

Silence smells like a battered and tattered
dusty unread book.

Silence sounds like nothing
when you're sat in a classroom where there's no voices.

Lauren Taziker (10)
Singleton CE Primary School

Love

A pink bag of candyfloss all to myself.
Roses fluttering in the air, the sense of smell that's always there.
Smell of violets in the air, all the children playing there.
Taste of cinnamon on the Earth before the lady gave birth.
It feels like a cold snake round my neck.
It looks like red feathers falling off a peacock.
It reminds me of couples on the sofa watching TV.

Lucy Hilton (10)
Singleton CE Primary School

Silence

Silence is as white as a snowflake
dropping into the cold, snowy winter.
Silence is as black as a cold, lonely dungeon
in the pitch-black of night.
Silence tastes like the salty water of the sea.
It tastes like the rumble of an empty stomach.
It tastes like the white snow mushing in your mouth.
Silence looks like the sparkle of a wet spider's web.
Silence looks like a floating pale ghost
drifting around the castle.
Silence reminds me of a pitch-black dark night
sitting on a bench.
It smells like a damp, smelly, old graveyard.
It makes you feel sad.
Silence sounds like nothing!

Jordan Leighton (10)
Singleton CE Primary School

Silence

Silence looks like a cold and rotting dead body
as blood starts to drip out.
It feels like a damp and soggy black graveyard
that no one knows.
It sounds like a dark and peaceful room
when you're all alone.
Silence tastes like it's a rotting egg
and smells like a dusty, old unread book.
It reminds me of pure untouched snow
just waiting for children's feet.
The colour of silence is green grass
lightly sparkling with morning dew.

Jamie Fish (10)
Singleton CE Primary School

Love

Love is a long walk through a beautiful garden
at night, waiting to be seen by others.
It is an enchanted world of freedom
just waiting to be explored.
Love is the strength in your heart,
mind and soul and the courage inside yourself.
It is a pretty song waiting to be danced to.
Love is a poor man sitting on the street
who has just been given lots of money
and you are appreciated by him.
It smells like sticky toffee pudding that's
just come out of the oven.
Love feels like my guinea pig's soft fur
rubbing against my face.
It tastes like chocolate melting in my mouth.
Love is a lilac bedcover over me at night.
It sounds like a little happy family of bluebirds
singing in the early morning.
Love is your best friend, it is always there
but you just don't know it.

Laura Wood (10)
Singleton CE Primary School

Silence

It tastes like a soft white snowflake
melting in my mouth.
It looks like a horse galloping in the field.
Quietness is peaceful, quietness,
where people want to be alone.
It sounds like a sparkle of glitter
dropping on the paper.
The colour is a glamorous bright white colour.
It reminds me of my mum cuddling me
when I'm upset.

Victoria Birkett (10)
Singleton CE Primary School

Fun

Fun is the colour of grass swaying in the breeze.
Fun is white, as white as a cloud.
Fun sounds like children screaming on a roller coaster.
Fun sounds like my kittens miaowing.
Fun smells like melted chocolate in a warm bowl.
Fun smells like a cup of tea just been made.
Fun feels like running on an athletic track
With the breeze going through my hair.
Fun feels like doing a dive in a swimming pool.
Fun looks like a funfair with the biggest ride in the world.
Fun looks like driving round the world in a car.
Fun reminds me of driving in a soft-top car with the wind in my face.
Fun reminds me of scoring the winning goal.
Fun tastes like cold ice cream freezing up your mouth.

Richard Booth (9)
Singleton CE Primary School

Love

Love is a bird flying through the air,
singing beautiful songs.
It's a sunset taking place in the distance
in the deep blue sky.
Love sounds like a saxophone
playing alone in the distance.
It smells like freshly grown
adorable roses.
Love feels like a warm, bright
light glowing in my body.
It tastes like a bowl of strawberries
just picked from Spain.
Love is golden bells ringing my love forever.

Hattie Pridmore (10)
Singleton CE Primary School

Love

Love's colour is sweet and soft,
it shines like the gleaming glistening sun.

Love's sound doesn't listen,
it speaks and says, 'I'm like the seven
seas crossing and crashing.'

Love's smell is as sweet as a rose
and as kind as its petals.
It smells like the first smell of hot chocolate.

Love's taste is like mouth-watering Belgian
chocolate as it melts in your chocolate-covered mouth.

Love's feel is strong and weak,
Its strength is hard lightning bolts
but its weak side is made of strength in your heart.

Love's look, well, it's invisible,
you can't see it but you know it's there,
when you can feel it.

Love reminds me of a silk sunset
over the high hills and gigantic mountains,
a creamy baby-blue sky,
it's not about money or riches,
it's about what's inside of your heart.

Rebecca Macdonald (11)
Singleton CE Primary School

Love

Love is the colour of the light blue sky.
Love sounds like birds tweeting in fresh green trees.
Love smells like roses growing slowly.
Love tastes like melted chocolate dripping in your mouth.
Love feels like the strong wind blowing in your face.
Love looks like a countryside picture.
Love reminds me of the sunset next to the light blue sea.

Lawrence Berry (10)
Singleton CE Primary School

Darkness

Darkness is black like the night-time sky
Fluttering through your bedroom window.
It sounds like cars rushing down the streets.
Darkness tastes like yummy blackjacks, waiting to be served.
It smells like burnt sausages in the oven.
Darkness looks like tall buildings in the city.
It feels like rough walls in the alleys.
Darkness reminds me of sleeping in my bed.

Samuel Sandham (8)
Singleton CE Primary School

Hate

Hate feels like the smell of dead roses in the air.
It reminds me of the gloomy look people give me.
It is the colour of black, like hatred.
It sounds like my heart beating in the dark haunted library.
It tastes like a dark memory that you would like to forget.
It smells like the hatred in my heart.
It looks like a hole in the middle of nowhere.

Rhianne Wilson (10)
Singleton CE Primary School

Fear

Fear is black, it is like a cold hand on your back.
Fear sounds like thunder, it looks like lightning.
It feels like a shiver down my spine.
It tastes like a hot drink.
It smells like smoke on a bonfire.
It reminds me of when my brother was born.

Jordan Bamber (8)
Singleton CE Primary School

Silence

Silence is the colour of silver.
It sounds like dripping wet water,
Dripping on your head.
It tastes like little snowflakes
Slowly dropping on the ground.
It smells like sea water
And the rain drifting water away.
It looks like a dark black cloud
Hovering over me.
It reminds me of a black hole.

Emily Barrett (9)
Singleton CE Primary School

Love

Love is gold.
It sounds like ringing bells in the air.
It tastes like sweet little fairy cakes with icing on the top.
It smells like lovely fresh flowers in the back garden.
Love looks like a big heart floating about.
It feels like a tingle inside.
It reminds me of hugging my mum and dad.

Emma Dewhurst (8)
Singleton CE Primary School

Anger

A volcano is red, but very hot.
It smells like burnt toast.
It is that hot it can kill you.
Anger is a fierce volcano.
Anger reminds me of sewage.

Dan Collins (8)
Singleton CE Primary School

Sadness

Sadness is like a drop in the ocean,
It's all cold and dark inside.
It reminds me of down in the cellar,
All dingy and scary, frightening.
Sadness is all blowy, like wind rushing past.
Sadness empties my heart.
It sounds like being dug up from a grave.
Sadness tastes like water,
All plain and icy on your tongue.

Lucy Willman (8)
Singleton CE Primary School

Happiness

Happiness is golden.
It sounds like children playing in the park.
It tastes like a golden biscuit
And it smells like a rose.
It looks like a nice flower.
It feels like a bear.
It reminds me of Dad tickling my tum.

Paul Fretwell (8)
Singleton CE Primary School

Anger

Anger is dark red
It makes me feel bad-tempered
Anger sounds like stones rumbling down a hill.
Anger tastes like burnt sausages.
Anger smells like rotten vegetables.
Anger looks like dark and cloudy skies.
Anger reminds me of stormy dark days.

Ruby Gratrix (8)
Singleton CE Primary School

Fun!

Fun is the colour of bright blue
Like the sunny morning sky.
It sounds like happy school children
Playing in the playground.
Fun tastes like home-made
Victoria sponge which my mum makes.
Fun smells like bacon sizzling in the frying pan.
It looks like hilarious clowns at the circus.
Fun feels like squishy modelling clay
Oozing through my fingers.
My friends remind me of fun.

Christian Powlesland (7)
Singleton CE Primary School

Love

Love is like a heart beating softly.
A heart is a rose colour.
A heart reminds me of love.
A heart makes thumping noises.
Love is like a heart.

Lily Jackson (8)
Singleton CE Primary School

Fear

Fear is a grey, grey tunnel.
It feels like a bee buzzing in your nose.
Fear tastes like bitter lemon tingling in your mouth.
Your heart bouncing up and down.
Fear reminds me of being angry with my mum.

Charlotte Mowbray (8)
Singleton CE Primary School

Happiness

Happiness is a wisp of smoke
Hovering in a golden yellow sphere
Making everyone around it warm and joyful
It's incomparable, it's like nothing else I've ever experienced
It's magic
Happiness is like camping out under the stars
On a cloudless night by a blazing fire, dozing off
It tastes like perfectly-made chocolate
Melting in your pinkish tongue
With caramel oozing out all the sides
Happiness smells like the reddest noses
On the first perfect dew
It sounds like the laughter of children
Playing on a warm summer's day
Happiness comes to anyone who wants it.

Ross Macdonald (11)
Singleton CE Primary School

Hair

Hair, you grow some, you lose some,
You sometimes don't grow any at all.
Your head will soon be like a ball
And then you won't be happy at all.

Losing hair

When you lose hair, your head shines bright,
You can't use a brush,
You will have a big fuss
And when you get older, you'll wait for it to grow back.

Growing hair

When you start to grow hair, it feels nice,
You play with it,
You mess with it,
Then you can put it up in a bobble.

Harriot Whelan (10)
Todmorden CE Primary School

Miss Looney Teacher

She's whirly and she's curly
And very fun at times,
But don't get her angry,
Or you'll be in for a big surprise.

She's coming and she's bubbling,
You've got her angry now.
It's not so often she's angry,
But she's really on one now.

Hey up, you've got her happy,
How did you manage that?
You have really got a talent,
Very good in fact.

She's roaring with laughter,
Let's try and calm her down,
It's no use trying, she's spilling everywhere,
Let's strap her down,
Hold her tight,
What's up with our teacher?

Sophie Mitchell (10)
Todmorden CE Primary School

Lights Out!

Oh no! Oh dear!
The lights are out,
You never know when
The ghosts are about.

Playing about
With the lights all night,
Do you know,
It really gives me a fright!

The very same night,
That I had that fright,
The ghost came to haunt me.

Carl Blakely (10)
Todmorden CE Primary School

Rats!

Rats in your bedroom,
Rats on the stairs,
Rats under your pillow,
At the side of your teddy bears.

So many rats,
Big fat rats,
Rats, rats, rats and more rats,
They're everywhere.

They drive you nuts,
They'll eat your crumbs, but leave dirty doodley,
The rat poison doesn't work,
These super rats are unbeatable.

So many rats,
Big fat rats,
Rats, rats, rats and more rats,
They're everywhere.

Underneath the sofa,
Rats, rats everywhere,
Up your nose,
In your hair.

So many rats,
Big fat rats,
Rats, rats, rats and more rats,
Will they ever go away?

Barry Cooper (10)
Todmorden CE Primary School

Crocodile

He lives in a swamp,
dwelling in the depths.
He owns the waters,
for everything fears him.

His eyes are yellow,
they give a cold stare.
His jaws are lined with teeth,
each are razor-sharp.

He feasts on snakes,
birds, turtles and occasionally humans.
His hunger never ceases,
so never get between him and his lunch.

He'll wait in the waters,
quiet and still.
Watching his prey,
then the chance will come.

Speeding out of the lake he'll charge,
mouth open wide.
Birds will take off, but the cattle
aren't quick enough.

Returning to the water,
he feels satisfied.
He won't be full for long,
soon he'll strike again.

Jacob Lomax (10)
Todmorden CE Primary School

Spaghetti

When push comes to shove
Spaghetti's the thing I love
It's tasty and yummy
It goes in my tummy

My grandma loves it too
Although it makes her use the loo
Spaghetti is so nice
I would never prefer rice

Now this is what I'm trying to say
I could eat spaghetti every day
I'll eat it for breakfast, dinner and tea
Spaghetti's the best I think, yes me!

Dannielle Westney (10)
Todmorden CE Primary School

The Lion Who Ate Our Teacher

One day we were learning
Our heads bowed down
Our teacher above us with a frown
A stealthy plod approached our door
A great big lion gave a roar

Its teeth were showing
All bright and sharp
And soon our teacher
Vanished with a harp.

Ian Gardiner (10)
Todmorden CE Primary School

Bad Food Exchanger

Love the food exchanger
He's your best friend
He changes all your rubbish foods
For all the good ones instead

Let him rule the world
For if he cannot rule the world
He swaps his job instead

He'll swap all the good ones for bad ones.

Jacob Colclough (10)
Todmorden CE Primary School

Hair

Linda and Helen, what a pair,
Both with long greasy hair
And have combs in their care.

Barry and Larry, what a pair,
Both have short, curly hair
And have gel in their care.

Isaac Pearson (10)
Todmorden CE Primary School

Mum And Dad's Food

Mum's food is delicious
Mum's food is sweet
Mum's food tastes like *chocolate sweets!*

Dad's food is horrid
Dad's food is sour
Dad's food tastes like *fish and flour!*

Bethany Whitcombe (10)
Todmorden CE Primary School

Yummy Or Disgusting

Jelly and mustard,
Old runny custard.
Gorgeous sticky buns,
Gravy that runs.

Potatoes that look cruel,
Porridge that tastes like gruel.
A mouldy pea will give you stomach ache,
Glasses of water the size of lakes.

Yummy, scrummy, delicious cakes,
Mouldy bananas that look like shakes.
School dinners will give you a fright,
So please, please, stay alive and don't take a bite.

Eve Brandon (10)
Todmorden CE Primary School

My Mum's Cooking

Breakfast in the morning,
Dinner in the night,
How I love the taste of a Frosties bite,
But when my mum is cooking,
I really don't feel right,
Because when my mum is cooking,
I really have a fright,
She always burns the lot
And it's hardly ever hot,
So that is why I'll have a fright,
When my mum cooks tonight.

Jamie Crampton (10)
Todmorden CE Primary School

Food Called Pizza

Food is delicious
I love it so much
Especially sprouts
And chicken

When I get food
I eat it up
Down it goes
As I lick my lips

My favourite food
Is so yummy
You've guessed it
It's pizza.

Jack Garbett (10)
Todmorden CE Primary School

Toy Store

Creeping down the aisles,
Jumping up the stairs,
Living toys everywhere.

Everywhere you look,
North, east, south, west,
They are there,
Surrounding you.

Creeping down the aisles,
Jumping up the stairs,
Living toys are
Where?

Jordan Hudson (10)
Todmorden CE Primary School

Lights Out!

Oh no! Oh dear!
The lights are out,
You never know
When the ghosts are about!

Playing about with
The lights all night,
Do you know it
Really gives me a fright!

The very same night
That I had that fright,
The ghosts came to haunt,
My, that was daunting!

Sophie Lord (10)
Todmorden CE Primary School

Spiders!

I slept at my friend's one night
Until I found out about those horrid little things
Spiders!
Spiders everywhere, in your ears, in your hair
They creep everywhere
In your bed
On the window
On the door
On the ceiling
On the floor
On the wall
That's where they crawl.

Megan McGuinn (10)
Todmorden CE Primary School

Lights Out

When the lights go out,
The screams come out and about,
Ready to shout.
Then I hear them screaming,
I know what it's meaning,
When the screams come out.

When we hear the screeches,
Coming from the streets,
When we hear the screaming
Of the baby's beats.

Billy McCubbin & Matthew Goldthorpe (10)
Todmorden CE Primary School

Blind

Where am I going?
I don't know,
Unsafe in the dark,
Going so slow.

Whispers all around me,
It feels so strange,
Now I've lost my sight,
Everything's changed.

What is happening?
It's not right,
Cold and shivery,
Where's the light?

Unsafe, unnormal,
Everything's quiet,
Hearing footsteps from
Children running riot.

Jodie Bamford (10)
Trinity & St Michael's CE Primary School

Uncle Steve

Uncle Steve,
Uncle Steve,
Your eyes are as black as mud,
Your ears have lots of studs.

Scary,
Scary,
Is your old shuttered house,
The curtains are as quiet as a mouse.

Mysterious,
Mysterious,
Is your little black cat,
Your hair is like a woolly mat.

Soft,
Soft,
Are the walls in your shed,
The shutters move like they're being led.

They say you're terrible in every way,
Then why don't you move, move far away?

William Booth (10)
Trinity & St Michael's CE Primary School

Monday's Child Is . . .

Monday's child is green and hairy
Tuesday's child can dance like a fairy
Wednesday's child likes red jelly
Thursday's child is rather smelly
Friday's child is the best
Saturday's child doesn't wear a vest
But the child that is born on the Sabbath Day
Is the greatest in every way.

Joe Grice (7)
Trinity & St Michael's CE Primary School

Grandad Bobby

Grandad,
Grandad,
Why are you so grumpy?
You sit like a cat that is so lumpy!

Growling,
Growling,
You're always growling,
Everybody sees you prowling.

Sad,
Sad,
You always make people cry,
OK, at least you try.

Robbie Pilcher (9)
Trinity & St Michael's CE Primary School

Mrs Cox Had A Fox

Mrs Cox had a fox,
being silly in a box.
Mr Spratt's tabby cat
was sleeping with the smelly bat.
Miss Cahoots has various newts
swimming in her suits.
Mr Spry has Fred, his fly
sleeping in a smelly pie.
Mrs Groat shows off her stoat
being sick in a boat.
Mr Spares has got grizzly bears
eating honey under the stairs.

Aaron Jordan (7)
Trinity & St Michael's CE Primary School

Granny Jenny

Granny,
Granny,
Why are you so old?
And you're always cold (what's that about?)

Granny,
Granny,
You're very strange
And why do you live in an old shuttered grange?

Granny,
Granny,
You've got shaky bones
And please don't make such a horrible groan!

Granny,
Granny,
You make jumpers with your hair,
You always take such time and care.

Granny,
Granny,
You say you've seen Cupid,
People say you're very stupid.

Child,
Child,
Stop asking me questions,
I'm afraid I can't answer them all.

But Granny,
But Granny,
I need to know,
So please don't tell me to go.

Child,
Dear Child,
You know you have to go,
So go, go, *go!*

Lyndsey Smart (10)
Trinity & St Michael's CE Primary School

Grandma's Grave

Grandma's grave is grey and gloomy,
I miss her ever so much.
She was never strict, spiteful or selfish
And she was always there to clutch.

She started to get shockingly sick
And felt strange inside her coat.
Although she really didn't realise,
Cunning cancer was running through her throat.

So now she has passed away,
Her very only strife.
Grandma's grave is still grey and gloomy
And I will miss her for everlasting life.

Meghann Cheetham (8)
Trinity & St Michael's CE Primary School

Ashes To The Wind

Never weep, never cry
For I, I won't die
No matter what
I won't be shot

I shall fight on
Even when almost gone
If my voice echoes in the night
Don't be stunned, stunned of a tearful fright

If I should die
Burn me
And throw me to the midnight sky
Even though I won't die.

Victoria Bate (11)
Trinity & St Michael's CE Primary School

Big Brother

He's a boiling-up closet.
He's a storming gorilla.
He's the whole of Europe.
He's an electric guitar.
He's out of control.
He's a zooming cheetah.
He's a clumsy elephant.
He's a fearless knight
He's an angry thunderstorm
In the morning
That's my big brother.

Matthew Parker (10)
Winmarleigh CE School

Lizard Kennings

Bug hunter
Bird muncher
Food nicker
Cushion scratcher
Blanket ripper
Brew slurper
Fish taker
Meat licker.

Andrew Young (8)
Winmarleigh CE School

My Cousin

He's a soft furry chair,
He's a rabid lion,
He's a tidy old cupboard,
He's a brave knight,
He's a miniature germ,
He is the drum king,
He's chilled back in midday
When he goes out to play.

Jack Swindlehurst (9)
Winmarleigh CE School

The Snake

Meat-eater
Sideways-slitherer
Mouse-catcher
Bug-cruncher
Tongue-flicker
Skin-shredder
Flicker-ticker
Diamond-dodger.

Benjamin Parker (8)
Winmarleigh CE School